OPTIONS TRADING CRASH COURSE:

A Complete Beginner's Guide To Trade Options.
All You Need To Know About Swing And
Day Trading, Technical Analysis,
Passive Income, And Tips To Become
A Pro Trader.

Benjamin Hoffman

BENJAMIN HOFFMAN

Table Of Contents

Introduction

There are numerous avenues available for those that want to manage their wealth and make investments such as mutual funds, bonds, and stocks. However, the opportunities to invest don't end with such traditional investment options. Another powerful way to trade is called "day trading" or "trading options" – a very versatile method of making some money through trading.

So, what are these "options" and how are they different from traditional stock trading?

Let me first give a quick simple comparison; assume there are many traders, and stocks of company A are available in the market. The average price of good company stocks is quite high – let assume they are $200 for representational purposes.

Ideally, buying a share of such stocks of a given company, say 10 stocks of $200 each, which is a lot of money that not everyone has to invest. The person will have to raise $2,000, which is not always easy to do, even if many can afford it.

However, those that can afford it fall into the minority. The rest might as well consider "options".

After investing in the company's stocks, one sells a portion and all of the shares back in the market when the prices are suitable to either make a profit or to avoid complete loss. However, like any trade, no one can ever be sure of how the market sways, thus making trading stocks a very risky one. Now say the person gets to sell the shares for $210 each, then the profit will come up to $100. But most people don't sell at such a small profit and wait until the profit margin rises to at least double the stock's price. However, that could take 4 to 5 years or more, depending on the market conditions and how well the company is faring. It is not everybody's cup of tea to wait out that kind of time and there will be many who will remain restless. For these people "options" represent a good choice.

On the other hand, "options" allow the traders to skip the intermediate step of buying stocks and go directly to the making money part, allowing investors to get directly involved with trading without actually buying stocks! That's right, the person has a chance to deal in stocks without having to buy them, wait for them to grow in value and then sell them. It is possible to jump to the final step of trading in the market.

Therefore, an "option" is a solution to problems that many new traders face in the world of stocks. Not all new entrants will have the confidence to invest in stocks and will look for a safe place to start with. "Options" allow you to do a lot more than traditional stocks, you can gamble on a changing stock index from a shielded position, thus cushioning yourself in case there is a market crash. So, it is a safe bet to invest in stocks and avoid market risks.

However, as cozy as they may sound, "options" used in day trading also come with their own limitations and risks, which could leave one with heavy losses if not handled properly. As was said before, no investment is free from risks and "options" also come with their fair share. It would be foolish to think that just by opting for "options" will make a huge profit and become rich within a month. If it worked that way, then every other person would be a millionaire. It is far from impossible to convert your hundred-dollar bills into thousands, but it will require you to pay close attention and become better at trading.

"Options" are multifaceted, uncertain, contain risks and are not for everyone, which is the main reason why someone might advise you to keep away from the world of day trading. Well, but what is life without a little well-informed, calculated risk? No risk no gain - it's vital to take a little risk from time to time. You never know, you might make it big and live to speak about it! Whether you take the plunge to trade or not, isn't it better to know a little bit about an investment option, instead of being deceived into trading "options" without knowledge? You will have a better insight into what you need to do while trading "options".

By the end of this book, you'll have a basic idea of trading. You can even read further and start practicing to learn the tricks of the trade. Remember, all those traders out there did not start successful, -it's taken them years of experience to be where they are. You might think of it as being slightly daunting but if you use the right techniques, you will have a real chance to make it big in the world of stock trading.

An "option" is an agreement, which provides the buyer a legal entitlement (but not an obligation) to buy/sell at a precise value for a given stock on or before a specific date.

It is like insurance for a stock or a bond; however, the agreement is well defined with clear conditions and terms.

It might still be ambiguous, so let's take a real-life example to understand an "option". For example, you find a car that was likely to have been used in a Bond movie, but the authenticity is not verified yet. You would like to buy it; however, you do not have the necessary finance to buy the vehicle for another few weeks – say 2 weeks.

You agree with the car dealer that you can buy the car in 2 weeks for $x. The dealer agrees to it, but in return to this deal offered, you must pay an advance fee of $y.

At this point, two things could happen:

The car was indeed the original car used in the movie, which means the car price will now rise steeply to thousand dollars more than the originally agreed $x price. But because you already made a deal with the car dealer, he has to sell the car to you for $x, which means you can sell the car for the new higher price value and take the extra money for profit.

However, on the other side, if you find the car is not in a good condition needing a lot of repair and making it is almost valueless. You can decide not to buy the car, thus saving $x, however you will lose $y which you made as an initial payment.

Now the deal in that example can be mapped to "options", the car to the actual stock, and so forth, giving a clear picture of the exact benefits of trading options. First, it gives you the choice: you can always go back on a deal if you see that it will turn out lousy. "Options" are also called "derivatives" for this very reason, that is, an "option" derives its worth by relying on something else. Here, the result can be anything and you will have to trust your instinct. More than instinct, it is important to trust your judgment in understanding whether the stock will work out to be a good "bet". This can be hard to do in the beginning but can get easier as you go along.

Let us look at a monetary example for you to understand it better.

Suppose A offers you 100 shares of company XYZ for $50 each. So, he is expecting you to pay him $5,000 for them. But you tell him you will pay him $1000 in advance and pay the rest later, in say 2 weeks. He agrees and keeps the shares for you. During the two-weeks, you find out that the company is superb and that its share prices will rise due to favorable news breaking out. If you are meant to pay him in the week, the price per share has risen to $60. Now, you will still have to pay him the difference of the amount after deducting the $1m000 that you had already paid him. This is because he had agreed to give you the shares at $50 each, which means you got it at a great discount. You can then sell it at $60 and make a profit for it. However, if the price drops to $40 due to, let's say, bad news about the company doing the rounds, the seller will still demand $50 for the shares. But if you think it is not worth your money then you can refuse to pay it. Here, you will have to part with your $1,000 that you had paid as an advance but will have the chance to save $4,000 in the process. That refusal to pay is your "option". Your seller will always wish for the price to drop whereas you as a buyer will wish for the price to rise. In most cases, the price always rises, as there is a constant demand for shares in the market. But you never know when the prices might change direction as nothing is guaranteed in the stock market so it could go either way.

Understandably, you will have a lot of doubts in treading this path in the beginning and might need a lot of help in trusting this line of investment. In this next segment, we will look at why trading with "options" is a good choice for beginners.

CHAPTER 1:

What is Options Trading?

The first step to consider when engaging in options trading is to have a clear and accurate understanding of an option. Most people barely understand what the stock market is and how it operates, and options are a level above even that. In this chapter, we will lay a foundation for the rest of the book by helping you understand what options are, why they exist, and what the different types and characteristics of options are. Then we will detail in the rest of the book to learn everything you need to be able to trade options with success. Remember that all forms of investing and trading carry financial risk, and not everyone who invests or trades on the markets will succeed.

What Is an Option?

Options are not restricted to the stock market. The name option gives us a clue as to what these financial instruments are, however. An options contract is one which enables the buyer to have the *option* to do something. Options contracts can exist in any context where you are interested in buying something. The proverbial example that is used is the option to buy a new home.

Let's say that Jane is moving to her new job in Houston, Texas. She is interested in buying a new home in a good neighborhood that is reasonably close to her job. She has two kids, so she's also interested in buying a home in an area with a low crime rate and good schools.

She finds out that there is a new housing development near her job. She also finds out that it will take about 4 months to have a home ready to move in. Because of the high demand in the area, home prices are changing rapidly. She'd like to lock in a price for a home but wants to look around in the meantime. How can she do that? The answer is she can enter into an options contract with the developer.

The type of homes that Jane is interested in are currently going for $350,000. Jane tells the developer she is willing to buy a house at this price, but she needs 120 days to decide. The developer knows that prices are rapidly increasing, but to make a deal he offers the possibility for Jane to lock in a lot and home for $360,000. She must buy the home on or before the date the contract expires 120 days from the date, she signs it. If she fails to close by that time, the contract expires, and the developer is free to sell the lot to someone else at market prices.

Jane is not taking too much risk because she is not forced to buy the home; she has the option. If prices end up dropping, she can simply let the option contract expire. If prices stay about the same or keep rising, and she doesn't find another home she is interested in, Jane can go ahead and exercise her rights under the contract and buy the house for $360,000. This is true even if the price of new homes in the area has jumped to $400,000 when the contract expires. So, by locking in a price, Jane may have put herself in a position where she could save a significant amount of money yet get the home (investment) that she wanted.

While laws may vary based upon the given specific contract type, generally speaking, the contracts themselves can be bought and sold. The contract itself becomes valuable because of the *underlying* asset (in this case, the home), and the ability to buy that asset at the fixed price. In an environment of rising prices, this can provide a big advantage to buyers. In many cases, the buyers won't go through with the contract. Executing the contract is called *exercising* the contract. Of course, if home prices in the area were to rise to $400,000, it would be worth exercising this options contract.

Jane may not want to do so. Maybe she found a different home more to her liking. However, since the contract has obvious value, she could sell it to someone else. Ever since financial instruments were invented, secondary markets were created soon afterward, where people traded them. Options are no exception.

Since an option derives its value from an underlying asset that is not directly traded or even owned by the person who buys the option, it is called a *derivative.* The media often talks about derivatives as extremely exotic and complex, but it is nothing more than that. A derivative is a financial instrument or contract that derives its value from an underlying asset.

Options on Stocks

The basic concepts of options that we described above apply to options on stocks. Since we now understand those basic concepts, let's define the specifics of options contracts on stocks. It turns out that options contracts on stocks are slightly more complicated than what we've described so far, but it's not complicated if you take it step-by-step.

The first thing to note is the underlying. As far as options on stocks are concerned, its corresponding asset is 10 shares of a specific stock. That stock is a stock of a publicly traded company on a major stock exchange. Options on stocks also include index funds. So, you can trade options on Apple, Facebook, or Boeing. You can also trade options on SPY, DIA, and QQQ, which are exchange-traded funds for the most significant stock markets such as the Dow Jones Industrial Average, the Standard & Poors 500, and NASDAQ 100, respectively.

For example, using a home purchase, we only talked about the option for someone to buy the home – we never considered having the option to sell a home. But with stocks, both concepts are equally important. The most basic concept is imagining having an option that would give you the possibility of purchasing those 10 shares of a given stock at a pre-determined sale point on or before the contract's expiration date. This kind of deal is known as a *call option.*

You can see that in a market of rising prices, a call option favors the buyer. The potential buyer can lock in a price. If they choose to do so, if the price per share rises by a significant amount (and by significant we mean significant enough to earn a profit if you turned around and sold the shares on the market), the buyer can buy shares at a discount.

In an environment of rising prices, since the option contract would give buyers such an advantage, the contract itself becomes more valuable. With everything else remaining equal, the price of said contact will be going up in a market of rising prices. People will be bidding up the price as more investors excitedly want to get their hands on the option.

There are going to be two types of buyers in the marketplace. Some buyers are interested in getting a hold of the stock at a discount price. Others are simply hoping or anticipating that prices will continue rising, so they anticipate that the price of the option will be higher in the future. In other words, they want to buy the option, and then turn around and sell it for a higher price a few days or weeks later at a higher price to make a profit *from the option contract itself.*

When we are talking about anticipating making a profit from future price changes, this is called speculating. The term speculating is associated with *trading*, which can be defined as short term purchase and sale of a financial asset with the sole intent of generating profits. It is important to keep this concept distinct from *investing*. The first difference between trading and investing in the time frame. Trading is generally done on short-term time frames of one year or less. In contrast, investing generally means five years or more. Investing is a long-term commitment to something you believe in.

Of course, investors hope that their assets are going to increase in value as well. Otherwise, they wouldn't invest. But they are in it for the long haul and will not be getting rid of their assets soon after they acquire them. The reasons for investing often go beyond simple profit. Investors may be passionate about the companies they invest in and the products they offer or believe that the companies they invest in represent the economy's future. They may also take a broad view, and invest in index funds, based on the idea that the economy will grow with time.

It is crucial to have a clear understanding of the difference between trading and investing, and understanding what "speculating" is, as an options trader. As we'll see later, you might have to express that you understand the difference as an options trader to satisfy regulators.

Put options

Now let's turn our attention to the other major type of option on the equities market. The option we are going to be discussing is known as a "put option". This kind of contract entitles the buyer to acquire a set quantity of stock at a pre-determined sale point. That might appear to you as somewhat bizarre at first, so why would anyone want to do that? The answer is that put options are valuable to buyers in a market of declining prices. If the stock is dropping significantly below the fixed price agreed upon in the options contract, it makes sense to either do one. If you already own the shares, maybe you purchased them at a much higher price, and you want to limit your losses. In that case, a put option allows you to cut your losses at a given price point that may be significantly above the market valuation. You don't have to worry if the market price keeps dropping, you can sell your shares at a price agreed to in the contract at any time before it expires. So, in this case, a put option can be a form of insurance for a buyer who has invested in many shares.

It's also possible for speculators to profit. The first case is where you want to sell the stock. To do this, you wait until the stock price drops low enough to make a move on the option would be profitable. So, you buy the 100 shares and then sell them to exercise your rights under the option. Of course, the way this would work is to sell them to the originator of the options contract, who is obligated to honor the contract and buy the shares.

CHAPTER 2:

Basics of Trading

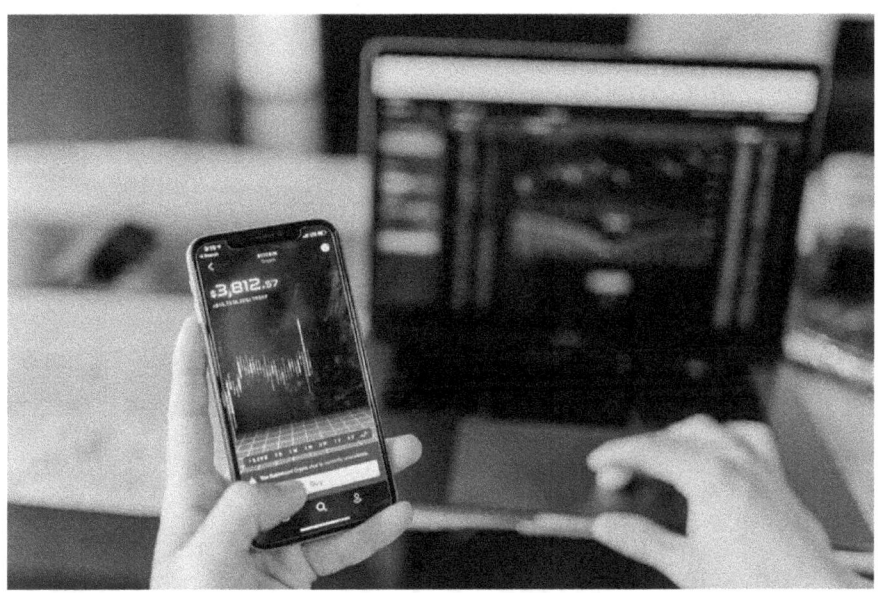

The main method for investing in the forex market, therefore, remains the classic forex market. When you operate on the forex market, you are buying and selling currencies.

However, other financial instruments have been introduced to invest in forex and currencies indices on the forex exchange over the years. We are talking about CFD (contract for difference) and binary options.

The main feature of these two financial instruments is the following: when you use them to invest in forex, you will not own the lots you invest in.

That said, for those who do not intend to trade online, it could make little sense. Let's try to clarify. Both CFDs and binary options are contracts between investors and brokers. It's not like the classic forex market, where traders buy and sell among themselves. In CFDs and binary options, the asset movement (in this case the buying and selling of currencies) does not occur.

CFDs and binary options are used to speculate on the performance of the value of equity securities. If the trader's forecast is correct, the operation will lead to a profit; vice versa, if the trader's prediction is wrong, the operation will lead to a loss. So, the mode of operation is similar to the stock market: if I invest on the upside, whether I do it with CFDs or buy currencies, I only earn money if the value increases.

CFDs are also derivative instruments, so they are used to speculate on the performance of asset values. This means that you will never own the asset traded (as opposed to classic forex trading).

Moreover, as with binary options, with CFDs it is possible to trade on:

- Equity securities
- Equity indices
- Forex currencies pairs
- Commodities
- ETF

The online trading strategies are based on mathematical and graphic analysis that can suggest the trader the best moment to buy and sell. As we have seen today, it is possible to invest in the stock market thanks to online trading, choosing between trading binary options and trading with the forex market.

It is evident right away that there is no suitable trading strategy for all traders, but there are different trading strategies, based on traders and their style of trading. Therefore, it is possible to customize different online trading strategies based on their trading objectives and their intellectual and psychological abilities.

We also recommend using 2 proven techniques not to turn winnings into losses:

Stop loss: it establishes a maximum loss that you are willing to suffer.

Take profit: you place a dynamic exit level that rises slowly.

Stocks vs. other investments

In this historical moment, the search for high returns has become almost spasmodic. Unfortunately, central banks' expansionary policy has caused the collapse of yields (now virtually 0). Anyone who wants to get a positive return must take risks.

In this context, many are deciding to invest in stocks. What we are wondering here in this chapter is whether it is worth investing in stocks. The answer? It certainly is worth it, but it all depends on the modality of the investment.

This is an investment that can still guarantee very high performance, provided, however, you follow some guidelines.

The first tip is to use only affordable platforms to invest in stocks. Among the best, we can remember Plus500 or Markets. These platforms are characterized by the fact that they are very easy to use, even for those who have never worked with the actions but, at the same time, guarantee advanced tools, suitable even for the most experienced traders and their needs. You receive a free bonus at the time of registration that amounts to 7,000 euros for Plus500 and 4,000 euros for Markets. This is additional capital that can operate on the stock markets but cannot be directly withdrawn. If you use the bonus and get profits, these profits can be taken without problems and constraints.

Both Plus500 and Markets are Trading Contracts for Difference (CFD) trading platforms: this is a particularly flexible and easy-to-understand derivative instrument that guarantees the possibility of obtaining high profits both when markets rise, and markets fall. This is the second condition that makes it worthwhile to invest in stocks: if you buy shares directly, you earn only when the markets go up. And in today's financial conditions, it's an immense gamble. It is not convenient to buy shares, the thing that must be done is to subscribe derivatives (such as CFDs that are very simple) that have underlying actions. Plus500 and Markets are the ideal solution for investing in stocks and, incidentally, they also allow investing in forex, indices, commodities, bitcoins, etc.

If you want to invest in shares and want to earn money, the advice is to open an account on Markets or Plus500.

The big advantage of stock investing: leverage

Through the use of financial leverage (or simply "leverage") a person can buy or sell financial assets for an amount higher than the capital held and, consequently, to benefit from a higher potential return than that deriving from a direct investment in the underlying and, conversely, to expose yourself to the risk of very significant losses.

Let's see how the concept of leverage works starting from a simple case. Let's assume you have $ 100 available to invest Leverage financial in a stock. Let's assume that the gain or loss expectations are equal to 30%: if things go well, we will have $ 130. Otherwise, we will have $ 70. This is a simple speculation in which we bet on a particular event.

In case we decide to risk more investing and our $ 100, with another $ 900 borrowed, then the investment would take a different articulation because we use a leverage of 10 to 1 (we invest $ 1000 having a capital initial only of 100). If things go well and the stock goes up 30%, we will receive $ 1300; we return the 900 borrowed with a gain of $ 300 on initial capital of 100. So, we get a 300% profit with a stock that gave a 30% return. Obviously, on the $ 900 borrowed we will have to pay interest, but the general principle remains valid: the leverage allows to increase the possible gains.

Considering the case further of the investment in derivatives. Let's assume we buy a derivative that, within a month, gives the right to buy 100 grams of gold at a price set today at $ 5,000. We could physically buy the gold with an outlay of 5000 $ and keep it waiting for the price to rise and then sell it back. If we decide instead to use derivatives, we don't need to have $ 5,000, but only the capital needed to buy the derivative. Let's say that a bank sells for 100 $ the derivative that allows us to buy the same 100 grams of gold in a month at $ 5,000. If in a month the gold is worth 5,500, we can buy it and sell it immediately, realizing a gain of 500 $. With the 100 $ of the derivative price, we make a profit of $ 400, or 400%, at $ 100.

Without using derivatives and leverage, the same $500, I could have earned them only against an investment of $ 5,000, making a profit of 10%.

What are the potentials of its use?

The potential of leveraging is clear. But be careful: the leverage multiplier effect, described with the previous examples, works even if the investment goes wrong. For example, if we decide to invest $ 100 in our possession plus an additional sum of $ 900 borrowed, if the stock depreciated by 30%, we would be left with only $ 700 in hand; having to return the $ 900 borrowed plus interest and considering the $ 100 of our initial investment we would have a loss of over $ 300 on an initial capital of $ 100. Therefore, as a percentage, the loss would be 300% against a reduction in the value of the share of 30%.

Another element to keep in mind is that the different financial levers can be combined: speculation operations are carried out using a "squared lever" with clear reflections on potential potentials.

What may appear to be an interesting tool with positive potential for the investor, on the other hand, presents risks that must be considered. Suppose the financial system as a whole works with a very high leverage and financial institutions lend money to each other to multiply the possible profits.

In that case, the loss of an individual investor can trigger a domino effect by infecting the entire financial market.

Banks are typically entities that operate with a more or less high degree of leverage: against a certain net capital, the total assets in which the resources are invested is generally much higher. For example, a bank with equity of $ 100 and leverage of 20 manages assets for $ 2,000. A loss of 1% of the assets entails the loss of 20% of the equity capital.

The development of the market for the transfer of credit risk (from financial intermediaries to the market) has meant that the traditional bank model, called "originate-and-hold" ("create and hold": the loan remains in the balance sheet until maturity in the bank that provided the loan), has been substituted for many operators from the "originate-to-distribute" ("create and distribute": the intermediary selects the debtors, but then transfers the loan to others, recovering the liquidity and the regulatory capital previously committed or the pure credit risk (credit derivatives), with benefits only on capital requirements), with the effect of a further increase in leverage.

The spread of this second bank model is one factor that explains the crisis triggered on the sub-prime mortgage market.

Property price inflation has supported the issuance of securitized loans and the exponential growth of the related market, allowing banks to make huge profits and, at the same time, increase leverage. But "the money machine" could not last long. In the end, many banks found themselves without sufficient capital to absorb the losses deriving from the inversion of the real estate market trend, resulting in fact as failed companies.

CHAPTER 3:

Basic Mistakes Beginners Make and How to Avoid Them

O ptions trading is every trader's point of interest, and you can make handsome profits from it too. If you have come this far in the book, you already know the potential that this field has, but it can be equally devastating for your career if you make the wrong trades. So, if you want to take this seriously, here are some mistakes that are commonly made, and once you know them beforehand, you will think twice before making them yourselves.

Not Having a Trading Plan

Not following any trading plan is probably the most common mistake of all, especially among the beginners. It might be that you read in some finance magazine that a particular company's stocks are performing well, or maybe you got a tip at a random gathering, and you decided to act it. Well, should you? The answer is both yes and no. No, because you should never take anyone on their word when it comes to trading. Yes, because it might turn out to be a good tip in certain cases, but you first have to perform a bit of research of your own and then decide whether that tip is worth believing in or not.

If you do not have a trading plan before diving into the world of options trading, it is simply as if you are driving your car, and you do not have a license. So, when you face a situation of crisis, the losses can be huge. In options, you do not have all the time in the world. There is a fixed amount of time within which you have to take action; otherwise, your option will expire worthless. You always have to be alert for any opportunities that might come your way, and if there is an opportunity, don't ever miss it. So, your goal of making a lot of money might not just be in your favor just because you did not plan for it. Remember that no matter how good your strategy is, sometimes they can fail when you do not have a trading plan.

Some of the things that your trading plan should possess are the type of options that you are particularly interested in like Nifty, equity, commodities, and so on, the amount of money that you can afford to invest in trading every month, the amount of money you want to invest in each trade, your risk appetite, and your expected returns from a trade. Make sure that this plan is followed for every trade that you conduct. You will be tempted to go off the track, but you have to resist those temptations and prevent yourself from risking too much. Your fear and greed both have to be controlled if you want to make it big. If you are just a beginner, start small and then work your way up to the top slowly and steadily.

Believing in the One-Size-Fits-All Concept

Selecting the strategy that would work best for you depending on the market's situation is what options trading is all about. Suppose you figured out a good strategy, and you have been using it for quite some time, and it is working out well for you. But that specific strategy is not meant for all types of trades. For example, you cannot use strategies of a bullish market in a bearish one. So, if you keep repeating your strategy without ever evaluating the trades, thinking that it will work like some magic wand and make you win every trade, then you are wrong. You have to learn to predict the market outlook and then choose the best strategy for you.

You have to perform technical analysis and fundamental analysis to find out which strategies you should use. Both macro and microeconomic factors have to be taken into consideration. Gather knowledge from different places by reading books and going to workshops. Read the views of experts from different reputed finance magazines. After you have figured out the market outlook, picking the right strategy would become much easier.

You have already read about the book's important strategies, and you know when you have to apply each of them.

Ignoring the Expiration Date

The expiration date of options is one of the major factors affecting our trades. As you know, to make profits you have to speculate on the direction of the stock movement. At the same time, I am also asking you to speculate how much time is it going to take a particular point because, in the case of options where your time is limited by expiration date, it cannot take you forever. Let us say that you researched and found some factors that can positively impact the stock price, but do you know when that price is going to reach the level you want it to reach?

Trading does not only mean looking after strategies. In the case of options, you have to look out for the expiration dates as well. Like the strategies, when it comes to the expiration date, you have many choices for it. Once you have gone through the previous point, you know that once you have built your market outlook, settling for the right expiration date kind of becomes the easy task. You should keep in your checklist some questions because then it becomes easier to figure it out. For example, you can ask yourself how much time you think a particular trade will need to play out. You can also ask yourself whether you want to hold a trade through major events or not like a stock split or a public announcement. Lastly, you should also ask yourself whether you have the required liquidity to pursue after this.

Overleveraging the Trades

It is always advised to beginners to get used to stock investment before you start options trading. When you have done stocks investing first, it is more likely for you to have handled huge amounts of money directly, and in fact, buying stocks directly also means that you have to pay the entire share price.

For this example, let us say that you are a person who can buy stocks worth $1000 at a time, and let's say that you have done this before but not in options. Now you have switched over to the options because of their affordable nature because they are a derivative. If you had to buy the underlying asset directly with all your money, it would have cost you way more money than what you're investing in purchasing the options. So, you don't need to invest a thousand dollars for purchasing that many amounts of stocks in the form of options contracts.

But this also poses a risk – a risk where you might end up overleveraging. Leverage is a powerful tool only when you use it wisely. Just because there is leverage doesn't mean that you should invest a bigger amount than necessary.

That is why there is a very common rule that is followed – consider it as a rule of thumb in your case. Try and limit your loss to within 5% for every trade that you do. You have to strictly abide by this so that all your capital is not lost behind any particular trade. When you lose only some money in a trade, you can always pick yourself back up and invest in a different trade, which brings me to the next point.

Error in Position Sizing of Your Trades

Two common emotions are responsible for all errors related to position sizing. These emotions are greed and fear. Suppose you are making a decision, and you become too greedy about your profits, you might position your trade too big so that it is not right for the size of your account. And this is even more common when your outlook of the market is wrong and then what you get in return is not profit but a crippling loss, recovering from which can become difficult.

This was just one mistake of position sizing. The other one is when you position your trade too small. There is nothing wrong with trading small, but do you know what it means? It means that you might not get the chance to make any substantial profit at all.

Here are some common ways in which you can maintain appropriate position sizing:

- Ensure the risk percentage for each trade is somewhere around 1-5% of your total account value.
- It is better for every trade that you stick to a consistent dollar value like $100 or $1000 based on how much you can afford to risk.

No matter what you do or which strategy you use, your position sizing should be such that you are comfortable risking that amount of money. In simpler terms, even if the trade does not happen like you predicted it to be, it won't hurt you to lose the money invested. In the ideal case, your trade value should be such that it is meaningful enough, but not too big that it has reason to make you lose your sleep at night.

Buying Options Based on Whether They Are Cheap or Not

Human beings tend to think that it is better to buy it whenever something is cheap rather than going for something costly. They think that this is the most cost-effective thing to do. But what you don't understand is that following this 'cheap' tactic is not going to help you with options. It is going to ruin your trade. It is usually said that an option tends to be more out-of-the-money when its premium is more towards the lower side. Yes, at first glance, it might appear to you that you have just found the biggest steal of your life but trust me when I say this, don't fall for the trap because even if you get it, making any money with the help of that option would be highly unlikely.

When the premiums of options are towards the lower side, those options' strike price is usually either well below or well above the market price. In simpler words, if you had to make money with such an option, then there has to be a miraculous change in the price for you to do so. So, let us say you bought a call option with a very low premium, and if you want to make money with it, it has to show a drastic movement upward. Similarly, there has to be a drastic movement downward if you want to make money after buying a put option with a low premium.

CHAPTER 4:

Why Trade Options?

I t's useful to know why we are trading options in the first place. The fact that they are cheap, is only one factor to consider. In this chapter, we will look at some of the specific benefits that come with trading options. Knowing what they are is going to help you make the right investment decisions.

Options Provide Leverage

When you buy an options contract, you control 100 shares of stock for that option's lifetime. The option is a tool that allows you to control those shares of stock without paying the full price for them. For example, Apple may be trading at $200 a share. An options contract on Apple might cost $125 for a particular strike price. Had I purchased the shares; the cost would be $200/share x 100 shares = $20,000. So, for 0.625% of the shares' price, I can control the shares for the time until the options contract either expires or I sell it.

Options are Inexpensive

OK, this is a restatement of the point above, but to buy shares you need a lot of money. Yes, you could buy one share of Apple, but if Apple's price goes up $1, what you've made is $1. To profit using stock shares, say by swing trading, you need to own a lot of stock shares. As we'll see in a minute price changes in the stock are magnified in the option. If Apple goes up $1, the options trader will be a lot better off than the guy who only buys one share with his $200.

Options Prices Change in Big Ways

The price or value of an option is directly related to the share price of the stock. It's not a one-to-one relationship in most cases, however. We'll see what the exact value is, but for now, let's say a call option for Apple stock will move in such a way that for every dollar Apple gains and losses, the price of the option will move by $0.80. This is on a per-share basis – so for the option overall, a $1 move in the stock means an $80 move in the option's value.

This cut both ways, so options trading is not for the faint of heart. It also requires discipline. If you are watching an option over a single day, you might see it go up and down by $50 in value if there is a lot of volatility.

But the advantage is that a small price increase in a stock can quickly lead to big profits. Suppose that you bought that Apple option for $125. If the price per share of Apple goes up $0.40, then the option's price would rise to $157. Had it gone up $1, the option would rise in price to $205.

Remember that goes both ways, so a decline in price by 40 cents would drop a $125 option to $93. Option prices can move fast throughout the day, so you have to keep a close eye on it, so you don't get wiped out and take advantage of opportunities to sell for profits.

Each option's price moves concerning the underlying stock price vary depending on the individual option. We will discuss how to figure out the possible price changes later.

Options Have a Higher ROI

The return on investment for an option is much higher than for stocks. Let's say you had $5,000 to invest, and we used that to buy Apple shares at $200 a share. That would give us 25 shares. If the price went up by $2, that would give us a $50 profit, ignoring commissions. So, we'd have an ROI of:

ROI = $50/$5,000 x 100 = 1%

That isn't a bad share increase for a single day move. Investors in stocks are looking for a return of maybe 8% *per year*.

We could buy 40 options contracts at $125 each. Using the previous example where a $1 move in the stock increases the per-share price of the option by $0.80 a $2 price increase would raise the option from $125 to

$285. The total profit per option contract is $160. Our net profit with $0 commissions on Robinhood would be $6,400. The ROI in the options case is:

ROI = $6,400/$5,000 x 100 = 128%

There are even bigger opportunities than this. On certain days you'll see stocks make big moves, like after an earnings announcement. The share price could go up $10 or $20 if earnings beat expectations. The opportunities for profits are enormous.

Options are Flexible

It's common to talk about call options because it is easier for beginners to understand, but put options give the options trader advantages a stock investor doesn't have. What if instead, the stock price of Apple dropped $2? In that case, the investor in the Apple stock would lose $50 instead. It's not a huge loss to be sure, but a loss is a loss.

But a clever options trader who saw the decline coming could have bought put options with their money. For the sake of simplicity, assuming that the price of the option was the same and it related to the stock price in the same way, the price of the put options would go up by $6,400 when the price of Apple dropped $2. And we'll see later that you can devise strategies that will earn profits no matter which way the stock price moves. These techniques go by the name of straddle, strangle, and iron condor, among others.

Options are Fast

Options have an expiration date. Some people will see this as a negative, but others will find it refreshing. Since options have an expiration date, they are not assets that you're going to hold onto very long (except for LEAPS). For those that like an asset with an expiration date, the result of this on a practical level is that with options, you will get in and get out of your trades pretty quickly. You might periodically do day trades when a stock is experiencing large price movements. I typically do 2-3 a week (remember don't do 4 a week unless you plan to deposit $25,000 and accept the day trader designation). In most cases, you'll hold the option for a couple of days and then sell it when the opportunity arises. If you are selling to open, you'll be holding the position anywhere from a week to a month or two. But there is no long-term investing.

CHAPTER 5:

The Right Mindset
Will Make a Difference

N ow we need to spend some time looking at the right mindset that you need to have to trade-in options. If your mind is in the wrong place, where you don't fully understand the risks and opportunities you are taking, it will make it hard to see profits. You need to be ready to take on the market and understand what is going on because options trading can be harder to work with than others. If you can keep your mind in the game, avoid letting your emotions take over, and come up with a good strategy along the way, you will find that it is a lot easier to see results with your trading.

Trading is more of a mental game than anything else. The best tactic or the technical indicators is going to be useful to help you spot a good way into the market. But they will be worthless if you do not bring in the right mental approach to the game. It all starts before you ever place any of your trades.

Being mindful the whole time you are in the trades, and even before you enter the trades, will keep your mind clear of any emotions that may get in the way. If you are a bit worried about how this will work and whether you are smart enough to go through these trades, there are a few simple questions that you need to ask yourself before you ever consider working with options contracts. The three main questions that you should consider include:

Why Am I Making This Trade?

When we get started with trading, no matter what kind of trading, there are a ton of strategies that you can use to make this successful. Things like price action and the fundamentals of the market can be enough to make anyone feel overwhelmed in no time. This is completely normal no matter who you are. No matter what tools we want to use, we have to make sure we remember why we got into the trade to start with, and then make sure you stick with these tools and only make trades that fit with your strategy.

Let's take a look at an example of how to make this happen. If you want to trade using the strategy known as moving average crossovers, you have to look at the charts and tools you have and see if any averages are crossing. If you want to trade options when there are periods with a lot more volatility, it is IV at a level that seems to make the most sense. There are a ton of strategies, and you can pick out the ones you like most. No matter which one you go with though, you have to make sure that you only place trades based on objective information. Never make a trade just to be in the market. Only be in the market and make a trade when it looks like it will make you money.

How Much Will I Risk on the Trade?

Risk management will be one of the most important things that you need to consider no matter what kind of investment you choose to work with.

Before choosing to place any trade, you need to figure out how much you are willing to risk on that trade. Knowing this risk from the beginning will make it easier to maintain objectivity during the trade, especially if it ends up not going the way you want. Never get into options or any kind of trade without really knowing about the risks.

Each trade should have a minimal amount of risk. The only way you can eliminate the risk is to make sure that you never enter the market. But the best way to lose all of your money is to take all that is in your account towards one trade without saving some back. Neither of these is good risk management strategies, so we need to find something that is a little bit better.

A good idea is to figure out what percentage of your account you are willing to risk each trade. It is best to stay under ten percent as a beginner. As your account starts to grow more, you may want to consider going with maybe three to five percent. You won't be able to put as much money towards the trades you do, but it can help you avoid risking too much and ending up with nothing to work with any longer.

When you keep your risk down to only ten percent, and sometimes less, of your account at a time, you will find that you aren't as emotional about the trades. Even if it goes south, your whole account is not lost. You can still enter into other trades, sometimes at the same time, without having to worry that your whole account will be wiped out with one wrong decision. Considering that even professional traders can have trouble with some of their trades occasionally, this is a good thing to remember.

How will I Manage My Trade?

During this process, we need to consider how we will manage our trades. If you find that a trade will move in your favor, think about how you plan to manage that trade. There are many theories of thought on this idea, and none are necessarily the best ones. Some work best for a few traders, others are preferred in some cases, and so on. You have to determine which one is best for you to help make sure you manage the trades well and get the profits you would like.

For example, many traders, new and professional, like to set up a profit target when they first enter a new trade.

Others will use trail stops to help them because it ensures they will capture some of the larger moves or larger trends that are potentially going to happen. Sometimes you may find yourself in a situation where you want to add to a winning position. This is more a personal preference, so you have to see what works best for you. But it is still critical to see how you would properly manage a winning strategy ahead of time. This ensures you make as much as possible without staying in the market so long you lose out.

The strategy you choose will make a big difference in how you manage your trade. A good strategy will help you know how to enter the market, and when it is time to exit. They can often help us learn how to read many of the charts out there, making it so much easier to pick the right time to get into the trade. If you pick a strategy, use the steps and tips it talks about to manage each trade you use it on. This helps to take the guesswork out and can help you get healthy profits.

While it may seem like these are really simple questions, and we shouldn't even need to ask them, remembering what they are and asking them during each trade will be the trick you need to make sure your options contracts are as successful as possible.

As a beginner, you may ask these questions of others and be surprised at how many never even think about them at all.

Consider the Emotions

As we go through all of this, we must make sure that we can accurately handle all of our emotions along the way. If our emotions start to come into the trade, we instantly lose all of that critical thinking and start making really poor decisions along the way. This is easy to do, which is why a good strategy and some strong stop-loss points can help.

We will talk more about these stop-loss points and strategies later on, but they allow you to make a good plan for your investment right from the beginning. You won't get caught up in emotions because you know exactly when to keep going and when to leave ahead of time. Before entering the trade, you have no skin in the game, so you aren't worried about things going well or things going poorly. You make sound and rational decisions, which will help you along the way. If you wait to make these decisions after you have entered, it is possible the emotions will sneak in and can ruin even the best trade.

CHAPTER 6:

Which Options Trading Platform to Use?

The following is a rundown of financiers and platforms that offer the best options for trading administrations. Peruse this list to see the stage that is most appropriate for your option trading needs.

TD Ameritrade

TD Ameritrade is in charge of the positions on account of its mix of attractive components like superb instruction assets, and a simple to utilize platform appropriate for traders with sensibly estimated administrations.

For each exchange, TD Ameritrade requires its clients to pay $6.95 and $0.75 for each agreement associated with the exchange. Brokers additionally get the chance to appreciate 60 days without commission ETF, value, and option trading to traders who place a store of $3,000 or more. The sans commission offer is accessible occasionally, and you have to check whether it is presently accessible. Other than these advantages, TD Ameritrade offers a couple of more rewards for customers with bigger opening stores.

Interactive Brokers

The Interactive Brokers platform has for quite some time been renowned for its ease of administrations. For quite a while, this platform was thought to have an unpredictable interface, and its client support was also problematic.

Only hyperactive traders could utilize this platform during that time. Today, the circumstances have changed, and Interactive Brokers presently stretches out its administrations to the less refined and the less dynamic traders. The organization's trading platform, called the Trader Workstation platform, is currently more amiable, simpler to modify, and accessible either as a site or an application. The portable application is very easy to use since clients can utilize voice orders and wheels to explore the screen.

Intuitive Brokers has additionally presented another component called the iBOT to its foundation. This application allows you to pose inquiries in English and find an immediate solution instead of experiencing various highlights on the platform to get a reaction. For instance, if you needed to see the strike price and the expiry date of a specific derivative, you just need to state, "Show options links for Company-X for the following two terminations."

Utilizing the iBOT platform, traders can likewise set up a spread rapidly, and afterward, extrapolate it into what's to come. The IB Probability Lab allows them to recreate potential exchanges before they can set down genuine cash.

Tragically, the IB platform only allows the spilling of its foundation in each gadget in turn. This means that you are using your portable application to stream statements on the off chance, and you open the equivalent on your PC, one of the platforms will consequently close, and you can no longer view the preview cites. Regarding expenses and commissions, account holders with under $100,000 store need to pay at least $10 every month and may likewise need to pay extra charges to see ongoing information. Dealers additionally pay a charge of $0.0005 per share. Another drawback of the platform is that its application structure comes up short on certain highlights.

Regardless of the drawbacks, Interactive Brokers is probably one of the best option trading platforms in light of its small edge rates, various instructive assets, and how anybody can utilize it to trade. There is no set least record balance or the irritating per-leg base expense.

Robinhood

The Robinson trading platform is profoundly positioned because incredibly, it doesn't charge any commission. For a trader looking to procure benefits, nothing beats free trading. Robinhood is a phenomenal application for novice brokers since it confines the dangers to which they are exposed. When using Robinhood you don't have to pay any trading fees, just chose the amount you want to trade and get started.

Even though Robinhood doesn't offer a lot regarding information and instructive material, the book's information will offer a good starting point for you to be able to use the trading platform on your own. This would be perfect for individuals who are just beginning option trading and pursuing it as hobbies or interests.

For traders who have taken up other venture vehicles like ETFs, stock exchanges, cryptographic forms of money, and ADRs (American Depository Receipts), Robinhood offers sans commission exchanges. Ultimately, since Robinhood is a web-first platform, dealers get constant updates about the state of the market, and they use this information to make trades in areas of their interest.

Lightspeed

This is an intermediary whose arrangement, the Livevol X, is intended to address experienced dynamic option traders' issues. T he platform additionally offers various explanatory devices like Skews Data and chronicled Option Greeks, which different platforms don't give. It also gives various systematic instruments that examine the market to get it together of various trading openings. Moreover, its diagramming highlights are progressed and simple to modify to your needs and preferences.

When you get onto this platform, you can examine your portfolio by gathering your options under specific symbols and images to decide the current dynamic methodologies.

The Lightspeed platform also accompanies a benefit and-misfortune chance diagram to help you measure the accomplishment of the methodologies you have chosen. During trading bursts, this specialist was accounted for to perform well overall and make trading simple.

Since Lightspeed is to some degree a muddled platform, option trading amateurs are encouraged to keep off it. The individuals who use it should likewise note that Lightspeed doesn't allow direct market access or prospects trading its foundation, both in the electronic and the portable application.

By and large, Lightspeed is an amazing platform due to its fantastic speed request execution programming that additionally creates diagrams to show value development. The per-contract commissions are exceptionally low, and there is no month to month or per-leg base charges.

Charles Schwab

The Charles Schwab financier runs a platform called the StreetSmart Edge. This platform is very easy to get either by downloading on your work computer or just logging in to the platform.

The StreetSmart Edge platform has various instruments and substances that help the client construct a spread by picking the kind of trade they want from its down-drop menu. Clients can likewise pick the legs from the options chain display included on the platform.

The Idea Hub allows clients to search for potential agreements passing by their potential productivity and market movement, and at that point categorizes them into four option specific classifications. The categories include secured calls, large movers, premium collecting, and profit.

When you see something you like, click on it, and if appropriate, click on Trade to dispatch your request ticket. On the off chance that your option is evaluated low, you get the opportunity to close it for nothing on this platform.

The Charles Schwab financier and its foundation are most appropriate for the intermediate options trader. You will just need to experience heaps of training and backing from the Schwab specialists. You additionally will appreciate the low expenses as well.

By and large, Charles Schwab stands apart on account of its Idea Hub which gives you signs regarding significant trading options in the market. It additionally offers to trade options that advance as you develop in your trading. Furthermore, the options depend on a wide exhibit of benefit classes.

The Charles Schwab financier and platform are a great option compared to other trading platforms for novice dealers.

CHAPTER 7:

Variety of Options and Related Styles

There are, of course, only two ways a stock can move, and one of these is a Call Option. A call bets that the stock will rise in price on or before the contract's ending date.

Available options come in many types and styles. We will overview some basic expressions that everyone interested in options trading should know and discuss all the existing option types.

Firstly, there are Call Options. These options provide you with the right to buy stock labeled as an underlying one. With Call Options, you can buy not only stocks but also commodities, bonds or any other instrument with a specified price, otherwise known as the strike price, within a specific timeframe. The Call Options contract gives you the right to buy, but you don't have an obligation. A bullish on the stock is usually the investor who expects the value of the stock to increase shortly. This kind of investor buys call options and manages them in the specified time frame. Again, let's take an example.

Let's say that the investor we will name Mister B thinks that next month CCC Company will have more significant earnings for the stock, and the stock will have a higher value. In this case, Mister B buys a call option for the CCC Company's stock for 20 dollars, for example. The option's contract has a term that Mr. B can buy up to 100 shares from CCC Company within the next two months. The strike price for these shares within this time frame is 100 dollars. So, if the stock's value goes below 100 dollars in the next period, Mr. B won't exercise his option.

It means that he will lose his first 20 dollars of investment (remember, if the option is not used within the specific time frame, or two months in this particular case, the contract expires and becomes worthless).

On the other hand, if the stock's value goes over 100 dollars, and the next price is 130 dollars, for example, Mr. B can exercise his option. He can now buy the stock for 100 dollars and sell it for 130 dollars on the market. The risk that Mr. B took paid off, and he earned a significant profit.

Secondly, we have Put Options. These options have opposite traits from the Call Options. Put Options represent the contract in which the purchaser has the right to sell his or her stocks. These stocks have to be sold for the strike price (a price specified for a specific time). Put Options, like Call Options, give the right to sell, but they are not obligatory. Now we can return to Mr. B and observe him as an investor who is bearish on a particular stock.

In this example, Mr. B thinks that the price of the stock he is interested in will decrease and, in that case, he will purchase a put option. According to Mr. B, the stock that CCC Company has is overpriced, and its value will go lower in the next two months. Let's say that Mr. B buys a Put Option on this stock for 20 dollars again. Contract of the Put Option gives Mr. B a chance to sell the stock he bought from CCC Company for 120 dollars in the next 60 days. So if the stock value increases more than 120 dollars per share, Mr. B won't have to exercise his Put Option, the time frame will pass, and the option will become worthless, which means that he would lose only his initial capital of 20 dollars. However, if the stock's value goes down, and the price goes from 120 dollars to 90 dollars, for example, the Put Option will be exercised, and Mr. B can sell this stock for 120 dollars per share. Once again, he judged correctly, and he has made a considerable profit.

How to Make a Profit Using Call Options and Put Options

There are many ways for a trader to use Call Options and Put Options and be successful in the process. The best way to show some of the most efficient ways to use these options is by using real numbers. Imagine you want to buy shares from US Bank. Let's suppose that the bank currently sells them for the price of 200 dollars per share and that you conclude that this number will go up since the shares are underpriced. Let's also suppose that the predicted amount of time the shares will need to increase their value is a few months. At the moment, you don't have enough capital to buy 100 shares from the US Bank. However, you still want to profit from the stock that will rise in value according to your estimation. If this is the case, you can use Call Option and buy it for the stock. This way, you reduce the cost, and you pay only a fraction of the original stock price. Now that you have purchased the Call Option, you have gained the right to buy 100 shares of US Bank stock for 200 dollars per share in the next two months. One of your first concerns might immediately be how you are supposed to buy that stock for 200 dollars per share in the next 60 days when you don't have the initial amount of money for that in the first place? Well, the thing is that you are not under obligation to buy the stock if you want to make money. If your estimation is correct, and in the next period, the value of the stock goes over 200 dollars per share, the Call Option that you bought would increase in value too. In other words, your option contract value rises with the value of the stock price.

Keeping this in mind, you get the opportunity to sell your Call Options contract to make money, not the shares. That is the real connection because once the stock price rises, your contract is worth a lot more than the money you invested in buying it.

A similar thing happens if you purchase the Put Options contract. The only difference is that your estimation has to be decreased in the stock value rather than prices going higher. Once the underlying security price goes down, the price of your Put Option will go up. The more that the stock price falls, the more expensive your contract becomes. Using options in both cases means that you can profit regardless of the rise or fall of the stock prices.

CALL: Buy, Sell, & Breakeven Price, Profit/Loss Chart

Long vs. Short

- *Long call:* this is the right to buy shares. This means you are bullish on the stock; you expect its value to increase, possibly by a significant amount.

- *Short call:* An obligation to sell a stock. It can be covered, meaning that you already own the shares (lower risk) or naked, which means you don't own the shares when you write the contract (high-risk trade).

Long Call (role: buyer)

For our long call, let's assume we have:

Long 1 ABC Aug 50 Call @ $1

This means the option contract is for 100 shares (the value 1 = 100 shares, or one option contract) of ABC stock. The option expires the third Friday in August. The strike price is $50, and the premium is $1. This is a low-risk strategy with your only risk limited to the premium, with high potential upside (though the probability of going above the strike price may not be high). It's also low risk for the seller since they keep the premium and the worst-case outcome is selling the shares at the strike price, which was higher than the price of the shares when the contract was written, but lower than the market price at the time of sale.

For the buyer of this contract:

- The maximum loss is limited to the premium, which is the quoted price multiplied by 100 for the total number of shares, or $1 x 100 = $100.
- Maximum gain: Theoretically unlimited, depending on how much the share price exceeds the strike price.

Short or Naked Calls (role: seller)

Short 1 ABC Jun 25 Call @ $2

This tells us that the option contract expires the third Friday in June. The strike price is $25, and the premium is $2. In this case:

- The breakeven point is strike price + option premium = $25 + $2 = $27.
- Maximum gain is 100 shares x premium = $200.
- Maximum loss is unlimited, depending on how high the stock goes because you would have to buy the shares if assigned. Since this is high risk and you'd need the capital available to take care of the deal if the need arises, brokerages assign levels to options traders to determine whether or not they are allowed to participate in such high-

risk trades. When you open an account to trade options, you'll need to know your assigned level to determine which types of trades you can make.

Put: Buy, Sell, & Breakeven Price, Profit/Loss Chart

Long vs. Short

- *Long put:* this is the right to sell shares of stock. You're bearish on the stock, but it's long because you expect to profit from the options contract by selling the shares at the strike price, which is higher than the share price on the market.
- *Short put:* This is an obligation to buy shares of stock. You're bullish on the stock and believe the share price will stay above the strike price.

Short Puts (role: seller)

Like a naked call, a short put is a risky trading strategy, and you'll be required to have capital available to risk. This is a small possible gain with a large possible loss option. Consider the following put:

Short 1 ABC Jul 30 Put @ $2

This option expires the third Friday in July, has a strike price of $30 and a premium of $2.

- *Maximum gain:* $2 premium x 100 shares = $200.
- *Maximum loss:* ($30 strike price - $2 premium) x 100 = $2,800.
- *Break-even:* ($30 strike price - $2 premium) = $28.

Long Put (role: buyer)

For a long put, we're betting that the stock price will drop below the strike price. We'll say our example is:

Long 1 ABC Sep 40 Put @ $3

The contract expires on the third Friday of September. The strike price is $40, and the premium is $3, so the cost to buy the contract is $3 x 100 = $300.

- Maximum loss: The maximum loss is the premium cost, so $3 x 100 = $300.
- Maximum gain: The maximum gain is given by (strike price – premium) x 100 = ($40 - $3) x 100 = $3,700.
- The breakeven point is the strike price minus the premium, or $40 - $3 = $37.

This is a lower risk strategy–since the maximum loss is much smaller than the potential gain.

CHAPTER 8:

How Prices are Determined

Before wandering into the universe of option trading, financial specialists ought to have a decent comprehension of the variables deciding the options' determination. These incorporate the present stock value, the inherent worth, time to lapse or the time worth, instability, loan fees, and money profits paid.

A few option valuation models use these parameters to decide the true value of an option. Of these, the Black-Scholes model is the most generally known. In numerous ways, options are much the same as some other theories—you have to comprehend what decides their cost to utilize them viably. Different models are likewise utilized, for example, the binomial model and the trinomial model.

We should begin with the key drivers of the cost of an option: momentum stock cost, inherent worth, time to lapse or time worth, and instability. The present stock price is genuinely clear. The development of the stock price up or down has a direct, however not equivalent, impact on the price of the option. As the price of stock rises, it is almost certain that a call option's cost will rise, and the cost of a put option will fall. If the stock price goes down, the opposite will doubtlessly happen to the calls and puts' cost.

The Black-Scholes Formula

The Black Scholes model is maybe the most popular choice for option pricing. The model's equation is inferred by increasing the stock price by the combined standard typical likelihood dissemination work. From that point, the net present worth (NPV) of the strike price duplicated by the combined standard typical conveyance is deducted from the subsequent estimation of the past computation.

Where:

C=Call option cost

S=Current stock (or other fundamental) cost

K=Strike price

Without r=risk loan cost

t=Time to development

N=A typical circulation

The math process with a differential equation that makes up the Black-Scholes algorithm can seem intimidating. Luckily, you don't have to know or even comprehend the math to utilize Black-Scholes processes in your calculations. Option traders and financial specialists use an assortment of online option calculating tools. Many present trading platforms gloat vigorous option valuation devices, including markers and spreadsheets that play out the counts and yield the option valuation results.

Beneath, we'll delve somewhat more in-depth into option pricing to comprehend what makes up its natural versus extraneous (time) value, which is more direct.

Characteristic Value

Characteristic value is the worth any given option would have on the off chance that it was practiced today. Fundamentally, the intrinsic worth is the sum by which the strike price of an option is productive or in-the-cash when contrasted with the stock's cost in the market. If the option's strike price isn't productive when contrasted with the cost of the stock, the option is said to be out-of-the-cash. If the strike price is equivalent to the stock's cost in the market, the option is said to be at-the-cash. Albeit characteristic worth includes the connection between the strike price and the stock's cost in the market, it doesn't represent how a lot (or how brief period) is staying until the option's termination—called the expiry. The measure of time staying on option affects the option's premium or valuation, which we'll investigate in the following segment. Intrinsic value is the part of an options price not lost or affected because of its length.

The Formula and Calculation of Intrinsic Value

The following are the conditions to ascertain the characteristic estimation of a call or put option:

Call Option Intrinsic Value=USC−CS

where:

USC=Underlying Stock's Current Price

CS=Call Strike Price

The intrinsic value mirrors the compelling money related bit of leeway coming about because of the prompt exercise of that option. Fundamentally, it is an option's base worth. Option trading at the cash or out of the cash, have no intrinsic worth.

Put Option Intrinsic Value=PS−USC

Where:

PS=Put Strike Price

Case of Intrinsic Value

For instance, suppose General Electric (GE) stock is selling at $34.80. The GE 30 call option would have a natural estimation of $4.80 ($34.80 - $30 = $4.80) because the option holder can practice the option to purchase GE shares at $30, at that point pivot and consequently sell them in the market for $34.80 for the benefit of $4.80.

The GE 35 call option would have a natural estimation of zero ($34.80 - $35 = - $0.20) because the characteristic worth can't be negative. Natural worth additionally works a similar route for a put option. For instance, a GE 30 put option would have a natural estimation of zero ($30 - $34.80 = - $4.80) because the intrinsic worth can't be negative. Then again, a GE 35 put option would have an intrinsic value of $0.20 ($35 - $34.80 = $0.20).

Time Value

Since option contracts have a limited time frame before they terminate, the measure of time remaining has a financial worth related to it—called time value. It is straightforwardly identified with how much time an option has until it lapses, just as the unpredictability, or variances, in the stock's price.

The more time an option has until it terminates, the more noteworthy it will wind up in cash. The time value of an option falls exponentially. The genuine induction of the time estimation of an option is a genuinely mind-boggling condition. When in doubt, an option will lose 33% of its value during the primary portion of its life and 66% during the second 50% of its life. This is a significant idea for financial specialists because the closer the option gets to lapse, the more a move in the hidden security is expected to affect the option's price.

The Formula and Calculation of Time Value

The equation beneath shows that time value is determined by deducting an option's premium from the characteristic value of choice.

Time Value=Option Price−Intrinsic Value

As such, the time value is what's left of the premium in the wake of computing the benefit between the strike price and stock's cost in the market. Thus, time value is frequently alluded to as an option's outward an incentive since time value is the sum by which the cost of an option surpasses the characteristic value.

Time value is the hazard premium; the option trader requires the option purchaser to purchase or sell the stock up to the date the option terminates.

It resembles a protection premium for the option; the higher the hazard, the higher the expense to purchase the option.

Case of Time Value

Taking a gander at the model above, if GE is trading at $34.80 and the one-month-to-termination GE 30 call option is trading at $5, the time estimation of option is $0.20 ($5.00 - $4.80 = $0.20).

In the interim, with GE exchanging at $34.80, a GE 30 call option exchanging at $6.85 with nine months to termination has a period estimation of $2.05. ($6.85 - $4.80 = $2.05). Notice the inherent worth is the equivalent; the distinction in the cost of a similar strike value option is the time value.

Instability

An option's time value is likewise exceptionally subject to the instability the market anticipates that the stock should show up to termination. Normally, stocks with high instability have a higher likelihood of being beneficial or in-the-cash by expiry. Accordingly, as a segment of the option's premium, the time value is regularly higher to make up for the expanded possibility that the stock's cost could move past the strike price and terminate in-the-cash. For stocks that are not expected to move a lot, the option's time value will be generally low.

One of the measurements used to gauge unstable stocks is called beta. Beta estimates the unpredictability of stock when contrasted with the general market. Unstable stocks will, in general, have high betas because of the vulnerability of the cost of the stock before the option lapses. Nonetheless, high beta stocks additionally convey more hazards than low-beta stocks. Instability is a twofold edged blade, which means it permits financial specialists the potential for huge returns; however, unpredictability can likewise prompt critical misfortunes.

The impact of unpredictability is, for the most part, abstract and hard to evaluate. Luckily, there are a few systems to help gauge unpredictability. To make this significantly intriguing, a few sorts of instability exist, with inferred and chronicled being the most noted. When speculators take a gander at unpredictability before, it is called either verifiable volatility or suggested volatility.

Verifiable Volatility

Verifiable volatility encourages you to decide the conceivable greatness of future moves of the fundamental stock. Measurably, 66% of all stock price events will occur inside give or take one standard deviation of the stock's move over a set period. Verifiable instability thinks back to show how unstable the market has been. This creates options for financial specialists to determine which option price is most suitable for deciding on a specific methodology.

Suggested Volatility

Suggested volatility is what is inferred by the present market prices and is used with hypothetical models. It helps set the present price of a current option and enables option traders to survey the trade capability. Suggested volatility estimates what options brokers expect future volatility will be. Suggested volatility is a marker of the present opinion of the market. This notion will be reflected in the options' price, helping traders survey the future volatility of the options and the stock dependent on current option prices.

Instances of How Options Are Priced

Below, you can see the GE model previously talked about. It shows GE's exchanging cost, a few strike prices, and the natural and time values for the call and put options. At the time of writing, General Electric was viewed as a stock with low volatility and had a beta of 0.49 for this model.

The table underneath contains the estimating for the two calls and puts lapsing in one month (a top segment of the table). The base area contains the price for the GE options that terminate in nine months.

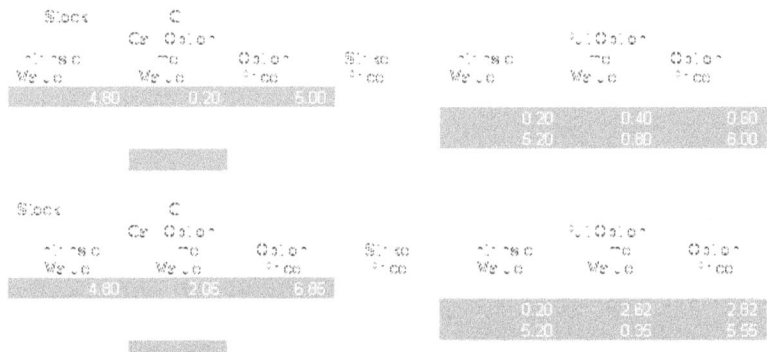

CHAPTER 9:

Money Management

What Is Money Management?

Money management is how you handle your finances, your savings, your expenditure, and investments. It is making sure you can survive a financial crisis. It means creating a budget for your long-term goals and making investments to help you achieve your goals successfully.

When you manage your money, you will be able to make wise purchases. Otherwise, you will always complain of having no money no matter how much your income is. It can also be known as *investment management*.

Money management is more about risk. When you have better money management skills, you will reduce the risk. You must understand all the areas of money management to be able to avoid any risks. Plan with a negative bias, always ask yourself 'what-if' scenarios; take action, and plan.

When budgeting for money management, make sure you are spending less than what you save. Excellent money management will help you monitor your spending before going beyond your budget. By doing this, you will secure your savings.

You will be able to invest if you make the right decisions. Avoiding taking on more risks will help you reach your financial goals. The strategies you use in your investments play a significant role in your success. Here are some of the basics, advantages, and disadvantages of money management.

The Advantages of Money Management

Better tracking of your money. When you have a reasonable budgeting plan, you can track how you use your money and monitor every expense. This is a significant profit to you, as you can spend less and save more money.

Monitor your expenses for some months, and then change your budgeting by removing the less required expenses and allocate that money to your savings plan, a retirement plan, or a vacation fund. Excellent money management will help you stay on track; you will be able to pay your bills on time, will be able to stay within your limit, and avoid bank account overdraws.

Poor money management can put you in bad debt quicker than the blink of an eye. You can prevent those nasty fee charges when you go over your limit. By having an excellent budgeting plan, you will avoid overspending.

A good retirement plan, better money management and savings plans will help you in the long term. You will be able to secure your future and have an excellent retirement plan. Better money management skills will give you a better retirement plan. No matter how much you save, even when you save and invest a small amount of money, it will provide you with a more significant amount for your retirement. Proper money management brings you peace of mind. Having bills on the counter and having no idea of how you will pay the bills, or not having the money to purchase something you needed is not ideal, but you can change that. All these issues can be difficult to face each day. By managing your money wisely, and experiencing all the profits of sound money management, you will enjoy peace of mind, and you can provide for yourself and your family, too.

The Disadvantages of Money Management

Rapid Changes

With the rapid changes in the financial world, it is important to change your management plans every once. It is sometimes challenging to adjust your planning to incorporate the fast-changing situations. Unless your plan can help to adopt the new techniques, it will be limited.

Time-Consuming

Managing your money can sometimes be a time-consuming exercise. It requires you to make the estimates, as accurate as possible. However, you can use software and mobile applications to assist you with planning, and this may reduce the time you will take if you were not using the technologies. And if you have less knowledge about money management, it will take you more time to achieve this.

Inaccuracy

When planning, you make a lot of assumptions in terms of estimation of your expenses. Any shift like an economic downturn or the change in the currency rate or interest rates can change your planning estimates.

Money Management Problems to Avoid

Research shows an increasingly growing interest in people learning about retirement and financial planning. This is excellent news; however, most people do not save enough for their retirement. About 18% are on the right track to reaching their income retirement goals and 4% average national saving rate, which is below 10-15% i.e. the recommended saving for retirement by financial planners.

It is very common to encounter some money management problems even after getting your finances together for many years. These problems can be significant and other times very simple; the everyday difficulties everyone gets at one point in their lives. However, by practicing and learning, you will be able to avoid these problems in the future.

The key is avoiding the money management problem, having peace of mind, and saving more money. Here are some of the problems that you should avoid to achieve a successful financial future:

Living from Paycheck to Paycheck

If you are already broke on Sunday and received your salary on Friday, then there is a huge problem. Try having enough money in your bank to take care of your living expenses for the coming 3-6 months. Ideally, you will have enough money for8-2 months to cover you during the hard times.

You will be required to set aside money from each paycheck and save it in the bank.

You can consider having a savings account so that you can make direct deposits. By doing this, you will avoid money problems in the future when you encounter issues, like the loss of a job, an illness, or a home renovation.

Spending More than What You Need

You probably dine out a little too often. Buying many lattes every week. Are you going to the movies a little too much? All these small things add a strain to your pocket in the long run. The small purchases add up to a high cost if you are charging them into your credit card.

You can choose other low-cost ways of achieving this, for example, making your lunch and coffee at home to minimize dining out or buying coffee every day. All these small changes will help you in the long run. Cut down on the needless expenses to avoid this money problem.

Poor Investment Choices

Looking for ways to make a lot of money faster, like the get rich quick schemes, will only put you into more debt. To make money, you have to save money even while in debt. You can consult a credit counselor to help you plan how to pay off your debt while staying on track with a smart budget.

Not Having a Savings Plan

You should have a budget and a saving plan, no matter your age or level of financial knowledge. Write down your finances and save the plan. Start tracking your net income. You can use mobile applications like Personal Capital, and create a saving spreadsheet. By doing this, you can know where you are overspending, that area you can save more, and make better financial decisions. Creating these spreadsheets will help you improve your finances.

Having Only One Source of Income

One thing that can bring money problems is having only one source of income. To be financially secured and successfully build a savings and retirement portfolio, you need to have more than one source of income.

For example, many very wealthy people have many income streams. Do not rely on the 9-5 work stability, only because the company might go down, and you will be left with no job and no source of income. You might have some savings to cover your expenses while you look for a job, but all this can be stressful. You can consider freelance work as a source of income, and you can start a blog or try out rental properties. Having a side hustle will help you a lot if you lose your full-time job and introduce new income streams even if you keep your day job.

Misusing Your Tax Return Money

Many people misuse their tax return money on needless expenses, forgetting to spend that money on their debts and other emergency savings. By saving this money, you will increase your savings and offer some relief to your debts. It might not be exciting, but you will be setting yourself up for a more secure financial position.

Money Management Strategy

This is about responsibly managing your money and having stable finances. Maximize your savings by implementing a money management strategy. The strategies range from *aggressive* to *passive*, and it all depends on your initial approach. Aggressive strategies include *greater leverage* and *broad profit goals*.

And passive strategies include *capital preservation*. Here are some of the money management strategies you should be aware of:

Budget and Adjust Accordingly

The first step in managing your finances is creating a budget. Many people ignore budgeting, because they find it hard to estimate their spending, and they have some numbers in their head to use a starting point. It is very common, though, for the actual numbers to be widely different. Budgeting will help you be more mindful of your spending and what you can do to improve it.

The more practical way is to know how much your income is and deduct the monthly fixed expenses. These expenses include rent, insurance, transport, and food.

These expenses are constant every month, so you can easily predict them. By creating a budget, you can compare your actual numbers and the monthly or yearly expenses. You will be able to have an accurate budget with time and experience.

Save For Retirement

Have a great investment plan, but do not forget to plan for your retirement. Find retirement plans where you can charge your retirement. Talk to a financial advisor or a bank and find out your options. You can decide to set up a SIMPLE 401(k), SIMPLE IRA, SEP-IRA, or employer-sponsored 401(k) plan.

Research these plans and choose the one that meets your retirement goals. You do not need to deposit a lot of money towards your retirement account. It will help you control your tax bill and tax-defer by saving over some time until you start accessing your retirement.

Establish an Emergency Fund

Having an emergency fund for your finances is essential to cover you during an emergency, like job loss and illness. Without an emergency fund, even small expenses like repairing a fried laptop will be impossible. You might decide to get a short-term loan to cover these expenses, but these loans carry a hefty interest rate. The short-term loan might help you to take care of the loan, but the cost will attract more cash issues in the long run.

Putting it into action, the hardest part is finding the money to create an emergency fund. From your income, find ways to cut costs or find an additional income source to make more money. Put the emergency fund in a savings account or find a money market account, but do not invest the money. This way, the money will be easily accessible when you require it. Start small and grow your emergency fund over time.

CHAPTER 10:

Basic Strategies for Options and Method

The next thing we need to look at is some of the different strategies you can use when you want to trade-in options. Everyone needs to enter the market with some good strategies ahead of time. This makes it easier for them to make sure they enter the market at the right times, and that they can also pick the right times to exit the market.

The Long Call

This is a strategy that bets the asset will rise above the strike price before the expiration date. If you look at the underlying asset and the market and you think the price will rise before the options contract ends, then the long call is a good one to use.

If you do this call well, then the upside on this call can provide you with an infinite amount of profits until the expiration, as long as that asset sees an increase in the price. Even if you see that the stock is moving in the wrong way, it is possible to salvage at least part of the premium you have by selling the call before it expires. The downside is a complete loss of the premium paid if the stock does not go up or starts to go down, but this is less risky than purchasing it outright.

The Long Put

The long put will be worth the most when you see the stock reaches $0 per share, so the maximal value will be the strike price multiplied 100 times the number of contracts you decide to do. You also benefit that if the asset price goes up, you can still sell the put and then save up some of the premium, as long as you still have a bit of time before your expiration. The most you can lose is all the loss of your premium based on how much you spend.

We want to use this one because the long put is a good way to wager on the asset declining. If you can stomach that you may potentially lose the whole premium, you can do this one. If you see a big decline in that asset, you will earn more with the puts than you would by short selling that stock.

The Short Put

The short put is seen as the opposite of the long put. The investor will sell their put, or they will go short. With this one, the investor is betting that the stock will stay flat or continue to rise until it reaches the expiration date. Remember that with this one, the other person is betting the price will go down and you hope it doesn't.

While a long call will bet that there will be a big increase in the value of a stock or other asset, the short put will be more modest and can pay off more modestly, though it can work in some situations.

Covered Calls

Another thing that we want to look at is the covered call. This is a good strategy because it will help reduce your risks of being alone on a long-term stock while making sure you can get some income in the process.

The trade-off that we will get with this one is that you need to be willing to sell off the shares you have at a set price, which will be the short strike price. Not sticking with this will cause you to lose money in the process. To help you execute this one, you need to purchase the underlying stock on the options contract, just like we talked about before. At the same time, we need to write, or sell, one of the call options on that same share.

Married Put

We can then move on to the second type of strategy that we can use within our options, and this one is known as the married put. In this strategy, the investor will purchase an asset, such as shares of a chosen stock. At the same time, they will purchase the put options for the same number of shares in that same stock.

The holder of the put option will then have the right to sell, within the time limits of the option, to sell the stock using that strike price, no matter what the stock's value is all about.

The reason that you, as an investor, would use this one is that it can help to protect them against any downside risk when they hold onto the stock. This strategy will then work just like an insurance policy and help establish the price floor if the price of the stock decides that it wants to turn and fall quickly.

Bull Call Spread

Now we can move on to a great strategy to learn about because it works well with options and in the stock market if you decide to purchase the stocks outright. With this strategy, known as the bull call spread, the investor will buy calls of an asset at a specific strike price, and then at the same time they will also buy the same number of calls, but at a strike price that is higher. Both of these will come with the same asset, so don't try to do it with two different ones, and they will have the same expiration with them.

Bear Put Spread

We spent some time talking about the bull call spread and how to use it when we think the market is bullish. But there are times when the market will go in the opposite direction, and we will end up with a bearish market instead. This is why working with a bear put spread could be the best option to help you out here.

Protective Collar

Sometimes it is a good idea to find ways to protect yourself in the market. It would be nice if the stock market, or any other underlying asset that you use with options, would follow a pattern that made sense and always stayed the same. But if that happened, then everyone would get into the market, and you would not be able to make the money you want. The good news is that the protective collar strategy will help you get this done, ensuring you are protected in the market.

The Long Straddle

You can't look much at the world of investing without looking at some of the straddle options out there. This is a great strategy that you can use to provide you with lots of choices and make it easier for you to stay

[109]

protected and make as much money as possible. We will spend some time looking at how to complete what is known as a long straddle. The long straddle strategy will be one where the investor can purchase the put and the call option simultaneously. You want to do this with the same asset underneath the option, with the same strike price and expiration date. Everything has to be the same on this one, except that you do one put option and one call option.

The Long Strangle

In the long strangle strategy, the investor will spend their time working on an out of the money call option, while also going through and doing an out of the money put option at the same time. We need to make sure the underlying asset of both is the same and that we keep the expiration date the same. This can help you to protect yourself if you are not certain which direction the market will go.

Long Call Butterfly Spread

This is a fun one that allows you to stay in the market a bit longer and can make it easier for you to see some results with what you are doing here. However, we have to make sure that we use it well and get in and out at the right parts along the way. The strategy we will talk about here is known as a long call butterfly spread. All of the other strategies we have taken a look at so far in this guidebook were a combination of two contracts or two positions. With this one, though, we will want to use the call options. With this one, the investor will combine both the bear spread, and the bull spread strategies earlier in this guidebook. You would also need to make sure you work with three strike prices that are different. You will still stick with the same expiration date and the same underlying assets along the way to make this happen.

Iron Condor

The next option that we are going to add to our list is known as the iron condor. This one is really interesting and allows us to work on many different things at once to see some results. The way to construct the iron condor is to sell one of your out of the money puts, and then we go through the process of selling one out of the money call while also buying one out of the money call, making sure we do this last one at a higher strike price.

Iron Butterfly Strategy

Then it is time to move on to a strategy that is known as the iron butterfly strategy. We talked about the iron condor and the butterfly spread, so now we get to have some fun and work with the iron butterfly strategy. To make this one work, the investor will need to sell one of the at the money puts and then they can buy an out of the money put, while also taking the time to sell one of the at the money calls and purchasing an out of the money call. This is a lot of steps, so make sure you know the market and how it is supposed to work before you start.

CHAPTER 11:

Market Volatility

As an options trader, you need to learn about the variables that can affect the price of an option and the ins and outs of implementing the right strategy. A stock trader who is familiar and good with predicting future stock price movement might think that shifting to options trading is easy, but it's not. There are three changing parameters than an options trader must deal with – the underlying stock's price, the time factor, and volatility. A change in any of these factors will affect the price of the option.

The price of an option is also called the premium, and the pricing is per share. The option seller receives the premium, which gives the buyer any right that comes with the option. The buyer is the one paying the premium to the seller, and they can exercise this right or just allow the option to expire without any worth in the end. The buyer is obliged to pay the premium whether the option is exercised or not, which means the seller will keep the premium, in the end, no matter what. Let's have a simple example. A buyer paid a seller for purchasing rights to stock ABC for 100 shares and a strike price at $60. The contract expires on June 19. If the option position becomes profitable, the option will be exercised by the buyer. If it does not seem to bear profit, the buyer can just let the contract expire. The seller then keeps the premium.

There are two sides to the premium of an option – its intrinsic and time value. You can compute an option's intrinsic value by getting the difference between the strike price and the stock price.

For the call option, it is the stock price minus the strike price. For the put option, it is the strike price minus the stock price.

To value an option, at least theoretically, you will need to consider multiple variables such as the underlying stock price, volatility, exercise price, time to expiration, and interest rate. These factors will provide you a good estimate on the fair value of an option that you can then incorporate into your strategy for maximum gains. The value of puts and calls are affected by underlying stock price movements straightforwardly. That means when the price of a stock rises, there should be a corresponding rise in call value as well since you can purchase the underlying stock at a reduced price compared to the market's, while there is price decrease in put. Conversely, there should be an increase in the value of put options when the stock price takes a dive and a decrease in the value of call options since the holder of the put option has the option to sell the stock at above-market prices. This pre-set price you can sell, or buy is called the strike price of the option or its exercise price. If the option's strike price gives you the advantage of selling or buying the stock at a cost that gives you immediate profit, that option is considered 'in the money.'

Time

Time is money. This adage still holds true and even applies to options trading. Thus, understanding how the Greek theta works is very important and affects the pricing of options. If you still remember, the Greek letter theta represents time decay on the value of an option. All options, call or put, lose their value as the contract expiration nears, but the value loss rate of an option contract is a function of the amount of time remaining before it expires.

The irrelevant part of the value of an option is the only factor affected by time decay. That means an option that's 'in the money' will have the same intrinsic value until the contract expires. For example, if a stock trades at $3, a call for a 30-strike price will retain its intrinsic value of $3 from the start until expiration. Still, any value that exceeds $3 is considered extrinsic value and will be affected by the time decay.

However, theta does change over time. Let's assume that a stock's price remains unchanged, a $2.75 'out of the money' option with a -0.15 theta will have a reduced value of $2.60 by the following day. The theta then may only be set to -0.12, which means the option's cost will be down to $2.48 the succeeding day if stock prices remain unchanged. The option's value will gradually approach zero while it's still 'out of the money.'

You also need to remember that theta's effect becomes more and more apparent as the expiration nears. You should anticipate a rapid acceleration of the time decay within the remaining few days before the contract expires.

Options that are 'at the money' possess the highest value, extrinsically. That's why these options have their thetas set to highest. Deep options 'in the money' or 'out of the money' have their thetas lower because 'at the money options,' they have lower extrinsic values. And the less extrinsic value an option has, the less they will lose as time decays.

The only way for the theta position to be positive is to have short options. This is because short option positions work best when the market is stable. Wide swings both up or down hurt option positions and only time will help as it passes by.

Other strategies also benefit from time's passage, such as neutral strategies, e.g., long butterfly. The less time there is before the contract expires, the less probability for the underlying stock to rise up or go down and reach unprofitable territories.

There will always be a trade-off between market movement and time for every option position. It's impossible to benefit from the two at the same time. If time is helping your option position, it will be negatively affected by the price movement.

Volatility

Volatility affects most investment forms to some degree, and as an option trader, you should be familiar with this element and how it affects options pricing. By definition, volatility is the tendency of something to fluctuate or change significantly. In general investment, volatility refers to the rate a financial instrument price rises or falls.

A low volatility financial instrument has a price that is relatively stable. Conversely, a high volatility financial instrument is prone to dramatic price changes, either way. In general, financial market volatility can be broadly measured.

So, when the market becomes difficult to predict, and prices keep on regularly and rapidly changing, the market is volatile Volatility can affect option pricing significantly. Many beginning options traders tend to ignore the implications which can lead to huge investment losses.

Historical Volatility

Historical or statistical volatility is used to measure the changes in the price of the underlying option, so it's based on actual and real data. Let's refer to it as HV for the rest. HV shows how fast the stock price has moved.

The higher HV is, the more the stock price has moved during a certain period.

So, when a stock has a high HV, the price is more likely to move, at least theoretically. It's more of a future movement indication and not a real guarantee.

On the other hand, a low HV might indicate the stock price hasn't moved much, but it might be going in one direction steadily.

You can use HV to predict somewhat how much a security's price will change based on how fast it changed in the past, but you can't use it to predict an actual trend.

HV is measured over a certain period, such as a week, month, or year and you can compute for it in various ways.

Implied Volatility

Another type of volatility that options traders should be aware of if implied volatility or IV. Whereas HV measures a security's past volatility, IV is more of an estimate of its future volatility.

IV is a projection of how fast and how much the stock price is likely to change in price. Many beginning traders focus on the profitability (difference in strike price and stock price) and the contract expiration when considering an option's price, but IV also plays a major role.

You can determine an option's IV by considering factors such as the stock and strike prices, length of time before expiration, current interest rate, and HV. Since an option's IV may indicate how much the stock will change in price, the price gets higher when the IV itself increases.

Because theoretically, more profit can be gained when there are dramatic movements in the price of the underlying stock. The price of an option can also changes significantly even when the price of the stock itself remains the same, and this is usually caused by its IV.

For example, ABC is about to release a new product, and speculations are building up that the company is about to announce it. The options IV for stock ABC can be very high since there are expectations of significant movement in the price of the underlying stock. The announcement might be received well, and the price of the stock might go up, or the audience will be disappointed with the new product, and stock prices can drop quickly. In this scenario, the price of the stock might not move significantly since investors will be waiting for the press release before buying or selling stocks. There will then be increased in extrinsic value for both puts and calls, rather than movement in the stock price. This is one way that IV can affect option pricing.

If you're betting that a stock's price will dramatically increase once that announcement has been made, you may purchase 'at the money' call options to maximize probable gains for that increase. If after ABC made the announcement and was received well, causing the stock prices to shoot up, then there would have been significant gains in the call options' intrinsic value. After the press release and the stock price movement, IV will then be lower since it's predicted that the stock price won't change so much very soon. There will then be a substantial fall on the calls' extrinsic value, and that would offset most of the profit you gained with the increased intrinsic value.

CHAPTER 12:

Important Trading Principles to Follow

You need to take it a step further by applying principles that will reinforce that plan. Think of that trading plan as the foundation of your house of success. The policies below are the bricks to develop your home into what you want it to be.

Ensure Good Money Management

Money is the tool that keeps the engine of the financial industry performing in good working order. You must learn to manage your money in a way that works for you instead of against you as an options day trader. It is an intricate part of maintaining your risk and increasing your profit. Money management is the process whereby monies are allocated for spending, budgeting, saving, investing, and other procedures.

Below you will find tips for managing your money so that you have maximum control of your options day trading career.

Money Management Tips for Options Traders

- Define money goals for the short term and the long term so that you can envision what you would like to save, invest, etc. Ensure that these are recorded and easily accessed. Your trading plan will help you define your money goals.
- Develop an accounting system. There is a wide range of software that can help with this, but it does not matter which one you use as long as you can establish records and efficiently track the flow of your money.

- Use the position sizing to manage your money. Position sizing is the process of determining how much money will be allocated to entering an options position. To do this effectively, allocate a smart percentage of your investment fund toward individual options. For example, it would be unwise to use 50% of your investment fund on one option. That is 50% of your capital that can potentially go down the drain if you make a loss in that position. A good percentage is using no more than 10% of your investment fund toward individual option positions. This percentage allocation will help you get through tough periods, which eventually happen, without having all your funds lost.
- Never, ever invest money that you cannot afford to lose. Do not let emotion override this principle and cloud your judgment.
- Spread your risks by diversifying your portfolio. You expand your portfolio by spreading your wealth by investing in different areas; add to your investments regularly, being aware of commissions at all times and knowing when to close a position.

- Develop the day trading styles and strategies that earn you a steady rate of return. Even if you use scalping where the returns are comparatively small, that constant flow of profit can add up big over time.

Ensure that Risks and Rewards Are Balanced

To ensure that losses are kept to a minimum and that returns are as high as they can be, options day traders should use the risk/reward ratio to determine each and to make adjustments, as necessary. The risk/reward ratio is an assessment used to show profit potential concerning potential losses. It requires knowing the potential risks and profits associated with an options trade. Potential risks are managed by using a stop-loss order. A stop-loss order is a command that allows you to exit a position in an options trade once a certain price threshold has reached.

Profit targeted using an established plan. Potential profit is calculated by finding the difference between the entry price and the target profit. It can be calculated by dividing the expected return on the options investment by the standard deviation.

Another way to manage risks and rewards is by diversifying your portfolio. Always spread your money across different assets, financial sectors, and geographies.

Ensure that these different facets of your portfolio are not closely related to each other so that if one goes down, they don't all fall.

Be smart about protecting and building your wealth.

Develop a Consistent Monthly Options Trading System

The aim of doing options trading is to have an overall winning options trading month.

That will not happen if you trade options here and there.

You cannot expect to see a huge profit at the end of the month if you only performed 2 or 3 transactions.

You need to have a high options trading frequency to up the chances of coming out winning every month. The only way to do that is to develop a system where you perform options trades at least five days a week.

Consider a Brokerage Firm That is Right for Your Level of Options Expertise

There are four essential factors that you need to consider when choosing a broker, and they are:

- The requirements for opening a cash and margin account.
- The unique services and features that the broker offers.
- The commission fees and other fees charged by the broker.
- The reputation and level of options expertise of the broker.

Let's take a look at these individual components to see how you can use them to power up your options day trading experience.

Broker Cash and Margin Accounts

Every options trader needs to open a cash account and margin account to be able to perform transactions. They are simply tools of the trade. A cash account is one that allows an options day trader to perform operations via being loaded with cash. Margin account facilitates transactions by allowing that to borrow money against the value of security in his or her account. Both of these types of accounts require that a minimum amount deposited. It can be as little as a few thousand dollars to tens of thousands of dollars, depending on the trader you have chosen. You need to be aware of the requirements when deliberating, which brokerage firm is right for you.

Broker Services and Features

There are different types of services and features available from various brokerage firms. For example, if an options trader would like to have an individual broker assigned to him or her to handle his or her account personally, then he or she will have to look for a full-service broker.

In this instance, the are minimum account requirements that need to meet. Also, commission fees and other fees are generally higher with these types of brokerage firms. While the prices are higher, it might be better for a beginner trader to have that full service dedicated to their needs and the learning curve.

On the other hand, if an options trader does not have the capital needed to meet the minimum requirements of a full-service broker or would prefer to be more in charge of his or her option trades, then there is the choice of going with a discount brokerage firm. The advantage to discount brokerage firms is that they tend to have lower commissions and fees. Most internet brokerage firms are discount brokers.

Other features that you need to consider when choosing a brokerage firm include:

- Whether or not the broker streams real-time quotes.
- The speed of execution for claims.
- The availability of bank wire services.
- The availability of monthly statements.
- How confirmations achieve, whether written or electronic.

Commissions and Other Fees

Commission fees paid when an options trader enters and exits positions. Every brokerage firm has its commission fees set up. These typically are developed around the level of account activity and the account size of the options trader.

These are not the only fees that an option trader needs to consider when considering brokerage firms. Many brokerage firms charge penalty fees for withdrawing funds and not maintaining minimum account balances—the existence of costs such as these cuts on options trader's profit margin. Payment of fees needs to be kept to a minimum to gain maximum income. As such, an options trader needs to be aware of all charges that exist and how they are applied when operating with a brokerage firm. It needs to be done before signing up.

Broker Reputation and Options Expertise

You do not want to be scammed out of your money because you chose the wrong brokerage firm. Therefore, you must choose a broker that has an established and long-standing reputation for trading options. You also want to deal with a brokerage firm that has excellent customer service, that can aid in laying the groundwork for negotiating reduced commissions and allows for flexibility. Option trading is a complex service, and your brokerage firm needs to be able to provide support when you are handling complicated transactions.

A list of reputable online brokerage firms includes:

- E*Trade
- OptionsXpress
- Scottrade
- Ameritrade
- Train Station

You can look up any of these brokerage websites and find that they have a long-standing reputation for quality service. Even though most based in the United States, many accept international accounts.

Ensure That Exits are Automated

Even though I have stated that emotions should be set aside when trading options, we are all human, and emotions are bound to come into the equation at some point. Knowing this is imperative that systems develop to minimize the impact of emotions. Having your exits automated is one such step that you can take to ensure that emotions are left out when dealing with options day trading. Using bracket orders facilitates this.

A bracket order is an instruction given when an options trader enters a new position that specifies a target or exit and stop-loss order that aligns with that.

This order ensures that a system set up to record two points — the goal for-profit and the maximum loss point that will tolerate before the stop-loss comes into effect. The execution of either order cancels the other.

CHAPTER 13:

Technical Analysis

How did you get into the stock market? Probably like almost all of us it was one too many tips from friends or relatives that made it clear to you: you should be there if you want to make something of your savings. But hardly anyone sat down beforehand and first rolled over specialist literature for a few weeks or months to get to know the essential disciplines of analysis.

You start and see what comes out of it. But soon, the moment will come when everyone will realize:

I have to take a closer look at that. And yes, you should do this to discover better strategies and assess opportunities and risks yourself. Because nobody wants to be surprised by the market, be it a super rally that you missed or a price slide that you got into entirely unprepared. But where should you get the necessary information from?

Technical Analysis - What Is It?

"Technical analysis," sounds like trying to connect measuring devices to the courses to check where there is a possible mistake. And that's not entirely wrong. It is about recognizing what is "in" the courses and deriving from them what this "is," which is hidden behind the pure courses, can mean for the future. Past price patterns tend to repeat themselves, especially since they are by no means miraculous, coincidental structures, but mostly logic. There is a lot to be found out that will give you greater planning security for your investments. But one thing has to be said in advance:

The stock exchange is not an exact science! Why not? Because it contains a component that ensures that it is only about shifting probabilities in your favor when you use technical analysis, but never about absolute security. And this component is the person, the investor, himself. Even if you consistently adhere to the signals provided by technical analysis, you always have to take into account that others may not do it, but act emotionally, from the gut. But even if the majority of investors act on emotions, technical analysis is still the best way for you to implement consistently. The charts provide you with information - because, in the end, this will always prevail over short-term irritation phases. Let's do it:

Trends: So, you have the opportunities behind you.

One can imagine what a trend is: Either the trend is upwards, sideways, or downwards. What does that help you to decide whether it is worth getting started or not? The basic statement is: If downward movements in each case return to rising prices at a higher level than before, this means that market participants are optimistic because they already found a stock, an index, a currency or a raw material at a higher price level as attractive and worth buying. This is classified as the last price drop.

In short: If you see such a picture in the course of the course, there is a positive mood - and of course, that is always good:

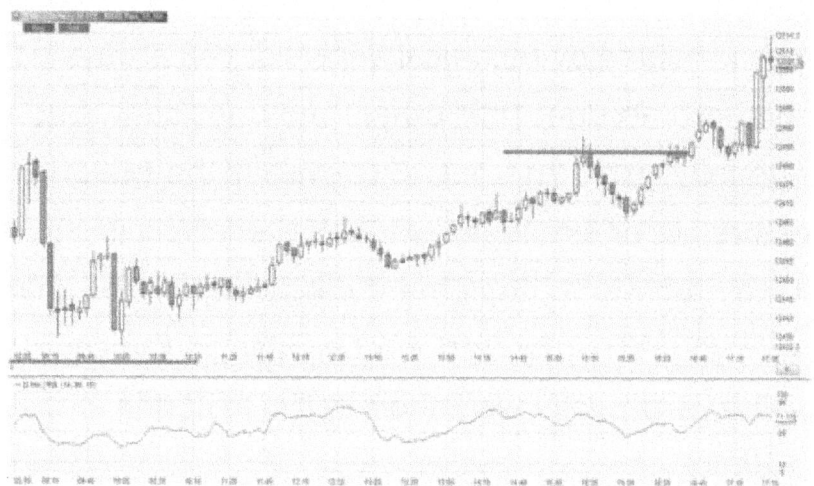

Higher Lows

Often you can also draw so-called trend lines. This means that when there is an upward trend, several reversal points are connected.

But be careful: Of course, you can always combine two points with a line, that is the nature of the matter.

However, only when there is a third point that is also on this line can a statement be made.

But then it is all the more important:

Upward Trend Line

Because if a third point arises - and then a fourth, even a fifth, which are all in the area of this upward trend line (there may be a little leeway as in this example. As I said: the stock exchange is not an exact science!), this makes it clear: The other market participants also see "your" uptrend line that they have identified as an opportunity to get in. So, it has become a crucial orientation. It is not for nothing that an old stock exchange rule, says:

"If you buy, you buy on the upward trend." Why? Because it would be a negative signal if this line, after becoming the beacon for an upward movement, is broken.

This means that close to an upward trend, you have the chance to get in at a relatively low price because a price decline precedes the test of such a line, and you also have the option of making your purchase particularly close via stop prices.

That means: Your chance is high, but the risk can be narrowed down.

If a line is confirmed several times, i.e., all investors recognize it and see it as an opportunity to enter, but the line breaks, something is wrong.

And then you should make sure that you leave the position first because if such a positive orientation falls, the mood regarding this stock, this index, etc. tend to change, and more investors get out.

Some of them may even be actively betting on falling prices, thereby pushing the prices even lower.

The following chart shows an example when such an upward trend breaks.

Trend Break

For downward trends, the above applies vice versa, so turn it upside down: if you find lower intermediate highs successively in a course, we have a downward trend. Investors sell earlier and earlier in rising prices, always below the last high.

This means that the majority assume that this previous high cannot be surpassed anyway and will, therefore, exit again beforehand.

As long as you don't speculate on falling prices as an advanced trader: stay away!

Downward trend

A note in between: We have shown the prices in so-called candlestick charts.

These are much more complex, meaning that they can be read and analyzed much more than a simple line chart that only connects the closing prices.

Trend channels

Trends become particularly engaging when they run in so-called channels. In addition to the actual trend line, there is a parallel to this. For upward trends above, for downward trends below the real base trend line. Such channels show that the market participants act in the direction of the pattern, but also always take profits with them.

However, as you can see in the following chart, this happens at ever-higher prices. If such a channel can be identified, it shows that the majority of market participants think and act fundamentally optimistically.

But they have recognized this channel and therefore also got out when the price came close to this upper limit and then will buy again when the lower limit of an uptrend channel is reached.

Upward Trend Channel

The rule also applies here: two points below and one point above always allow a channel to be drawn upward. Only when these three points have been confirmed, be it by a second point on the top and a third point on the base trend line is such a trend relevant because it is recognized and implemented by investors.

In between, it is precisely this "recognition" of the formations that is decisive. Trend lines, trend channels, and all other technical chart elements that you will get to know below are not a natural law. They are based on precisely this "recognition" of the players, i.e., the price behavior shows you as an investor that these formations have been recognized and that they are based on them: the market participants buy on a trend line, for example, because they assume that the other investors will do too.

Only when the behavior of investors confirms them are, they a great guide. This is also why there is only a manageable number of such formations that obey the general rules. If you started to create your structures from price histories that no one else knows or sees, the signals from your formation would hardly be successful because the other investors do not see "your" formation and therefore have no reason to get on or off.

Resistances and Supports

We haven't mentioned a trend yet: the sideways trend. As the name suggests, it is a sideways movement that can be squeezed into a fairly clear framework because the course changes in the course take place in a narrow area on the top and bottom.

From this, it follows that the market participants don't know how to proceed in the short term, or the majority think that the price should be where it is.

In such a situation, only a few would actively buy and sell, and this would result in a fluctuating movement that would lead sideways on balance.

Sideways Trend

The upper limit serves as resistance to a further increase; the lower limit is called support. This also applies to trends per se: wherever a course turns upwards, i.e., a turning point arises, this creates support. Wherever a price turns down, whether in a trend or somewhere in the middle of "nothing," i.e., outside of relevant trend lines, resistance arises.

At this turning point in the course of the price, buying interest has suddenly increased significantly. This point supports the price from this point on because market participants suspect that when the price returns to this point, those who bought there the first time could buy again. Which, for safety's sake, encourages you to stop selling yourself there and even buy it again if you suspect it. And so, the course often turns up back at such points, usually also a little above.

Here is a typical example:

Supports

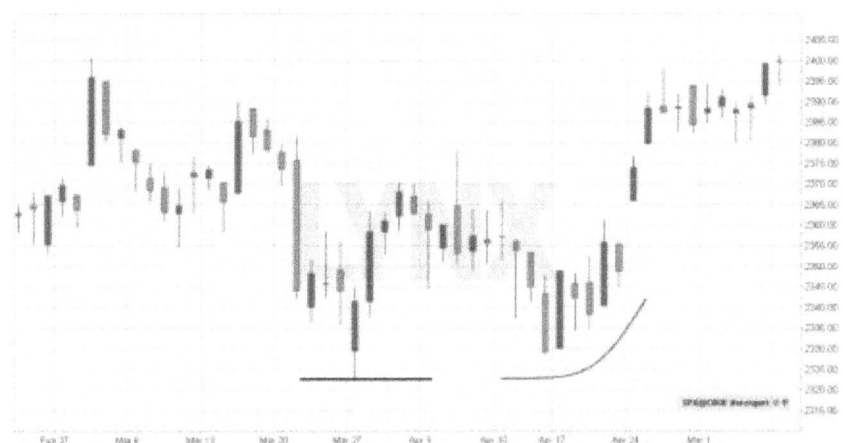

Conversely, this applies to resistances, such as those that limit a sideways trend upwards but can also appear in isolation somewhere in the course of the price.

There it is suspected that those who had sold at this level could exit again if this point is reached yet.

So many will only stop buying when this point gets closer.

Some speculative actors will actively work to make the course turn there and go short, so these turning points, whether resistance or support, can become a kind of self-fulfilling prophecy.

Resistances

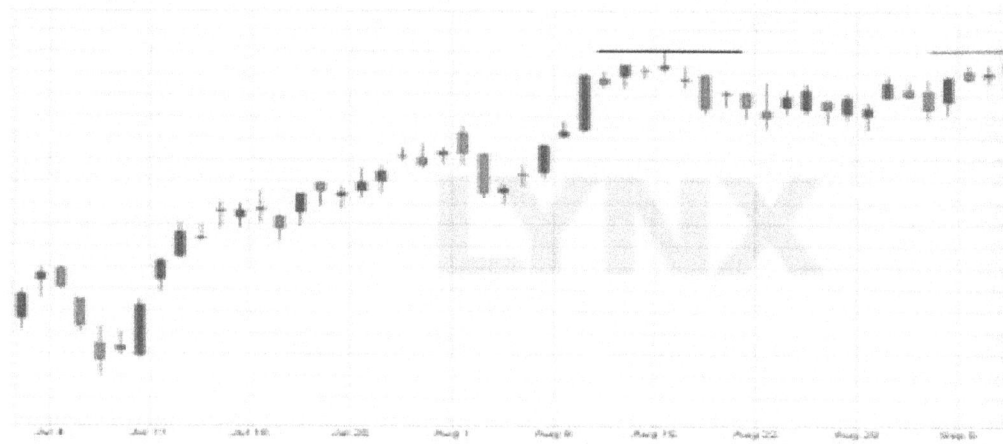

It also follows from this that breaking such support can have correspondingly marked consequences. If the expectation that the price will turn around at such a point is not met, many traders react immediately by either continuing their sales directly or existing positions, which they have usefully secured with a stop price below this turning point and in the event of holding the support, sell. The following chart provides an example.

Break of a support

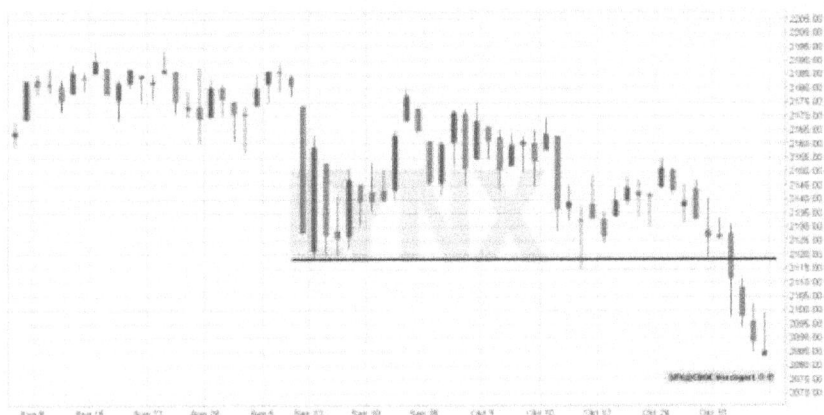

Conversely, resistance is overcome. If at a point where there was a downward turn in advance, suddenly there is no renewed selling pressure, but the price continues to go up, this is a positive signal: Those who had quit there now seem to no longer do so, So the way up seems free. With this, investors who had previously been cautious about this resistance are currently buying and are helping the price to overcome this hurdle more clearly.

CHAPTER 14:

Candlestick Charts

Candlestick charts weren't known in the West before the 1980s when they were introduced. However, Japan used this method for centuries, which at the same time makes Japan the place of origin of the candlestick method. As we have already seen before, these charts show the same information as the bar chart that was used before we started using the Japanese system. The reason that the candlestick charts became so popular in such a short amount of time is the fact that they are easier to understand and they use simple yet innovative body illustrations that helps the investor see every change at a glance. Let's recap some of the basic characteristics of the candlestick as the general pattern. Firstly, the total length of the candle represents the trading range for the predetermined period. The body of the candle is connected to the distance between the prices known as the closing price and the opening price. The difference in color shows if the price went up or down for a certain period. The length of the candle also portrays the volatility of the price, and the sum of the candle and the "body" of the candle can be viewed as the progress that was made for one day. If the chart shows that the candle's "body" is short, it means that the closing and the opening prices were close or similar. If that is the case, we can say that the buyers and the sellers were in balance.

Types

When it comes to the candlestick chart, there are regular candles and then there is Doji. Doji is a special candle whose body is just a horizontal line. This line represents closing prices and opening prices, which in case you have Doji are equivalent.

If the candles have long bodies, that will indicate that the trend of the price is strong. If your chart has candles without any wicks, it means that you got Marubozu. Marubozu is an indicator that shows that the trades were only made in the range of the opening and closing prices; thus, no trade was made outside of that range. This is a very strong indication, which means that the market was strongly pushing the price only in one direction.

1. Hammer

When it comes to ideal signals, in Hammer, that signal is represented with a small body. Its wick should be two times longer than the body regardless of the day being up or down for the price trend. Hammer sometimes signals that the trend of the price will reverse. The way to confirm such an assumption and make it actionable is to wait for the following day and see if the price is going to increase. If the price starts rising, it means that your interpretation of trend reversal has been confirmed. This pattern works because many trader's panic, and if the price is down for some time, they will sell at any price. If we try to express this situation in the candle chart, it means that the wick is going to be pushed down. However, smart investors come in, and they buy, which pushes the price up once again. These trend reversals can last through the whole day and even keep happening the following day too.

2. Hanging Man

The Hanging Man is a pattern that looks the same as the Hammer; the only difference is that it comes in an uptrend. Just like before, we search for a change in the price trend on the following day so we could confirm our estimation of the trend's reversal. The psychology, in this case, is that traders mostly decide to take profits. That way, they push the prices down. Still, some of those who are new on the market see this as their chance to buy. That way, they push the price back up. In any case, this candle is considered to be weak. As a reflection of this pattern, it appears that traders have a hunch that this means that the trend is over, so the selling starts to rise again in the following few days.

3. Inverted Hammer

Once you see the diagrams for the first two candlestick patterns, you will realize that the inverted hammer also has similar characteristics. There is also certain psychology behind the signaling, and we will briefly explain it. Once the downtrend starts weakening and several traders have second thoughts, they start buying, which pushes the prices up. Sellers also come back in the game, which means that the price will close down. However, if the price starts increasing during the following day, then the conclusion is that the weakness of the trend made buyers buy even more while pushing up the prices, and that way, the uptrend started.

4. Shooting Star

The last but not the least in the set of four related candle signals is the pattern known as the Shooting Star, which comes in an uptrend. Everybody knows that beginners or novices, if you prefer, tend to buy on the top. Shooting star simply demonstrates the exuberance that the future causes the traders to see the high wick that appears when novices enter the market. The traders who notice this are usually those who appeared thinking that it is time to sell. Just like in every other pattern above, the only way to confirm this is to wait for the following day and to determine if that was the signal that shows that the trend will reverse.

5. Bullish Engulfing

This is a pattern that consists of two candles, and it is graded as highly probable. When in a downtrend, the first candle pressures that the selling continues. The pressure is strong enough to allow the following candle to open up at an even lower price. But those investors who are smart see an opportunity here, and they start buying on the second candle in this case. This makes the price to grow and launches it above the limit of the preceding period. This is one of the numerous proofs that the real power is in the hands of the buyers and that there is a high possibility that the trend will reverse.

6. Bearish Engulfing

It has the same concept as bullish engulfing. The thing is that sometimes uptrend can stretch so badly that the opening price can go even higher than the current price in the earlier candle. Smart and experienced investors usually decide to sell on these occasions. The length of the candle, in this case, shows that the trend can be reversed from an uptrend to a downtrend due to the weight of an opinion.

7. Piercing Candle

Piercing candle is a pattern that represents a strong bearish candle that is in a downtrend. This candle, with another following candle, opens up at a price that is lower than the current one. However, the candle is rallying to have the finishing price, which has the same trading range as the earlier day. This pattern can be seen as a signal for the trend reversal, and the reason for that piercing candle is an indicator that sellers are feeling hopeless. When the low prices go even lower, it is an opportunity for those who consider themselves to be smart investors to start buying and to push prices strongly up.

8. Dark Cloud Cover

This is a pattern that has entirely the same characteristic as the piercing candle pattern. The only difference is that the dark cloud cover is in an uptrend.

9. Bullish Harami

This pattern has a name that originated from the Japanese word harami that means "pregnant." As the name suggests, the reason for this is that according to them, these candlestick patterns have a resemblance to the pregnant women. If you happen to encounter the bullish harami, it means that the market had a lot of active sellers. However, the other candle indicates that the current price became higher. If the second candle finishes up and provides enough buying pressure, you can see it as a signal that there is going to be a change in the price trend. As usual, the following day is a confirmation checker.

10.   Bearish Harami

When a pattern reaches the end of an uptrend, there can be a candle that demonstrates exuberance that some might see as naïve. When the other period opens up, and the price is lower and continuing to go lower as the day goes by, we can say that it indicates second thoughts in buyers. The most probable outcome of this situation is that the selling will continue as normal and that everything will be resolved once the price goes into a downtrend.

CHAPTER 15:

Risk Management

What is Risk Management?

Trading is generally not without risk and options pose a higher risk compared to other forms of securities. The risk is largely due to its speculative nature. As a trader, you need to protect yourself and trading capital from unnecessary losses and any potential losses that can be prevented.

As a trader, the first thing you need to think about is not losing money. We do not engage in trades in order to lose money. A lot of beginners lose money in their early days. Some believe that this is an inevitable process. However, it does not have to be this way. With proper planning and especially proper risk management, you should not unnecessarily lose money trading the markets.

In fact, to be successful as a trader, your number one focus should be risk management rather than winning trades or strategies. A good trader is one who does not unnecessarily lose money. The most successful traders are those who manage their funds so well they always know how much to spend or hold back. To do this, you have to watch your every move and countercheck every decision that you make. For instance, if you want to enter a position in the markets, you need to ask yourself if that move is necessary and what amounts you stand to lose should it not work out.

Effective Risk Management

The options trading process does carry some risks with it. Understanding these risks and taking mitigating steps will make you not just a better trader but a more profitable one as well. A lot of trader's love options trading because of the immense leverage that this kind of trading affords them. Should an investment work out as desired, then the profits are often quite high. With stocks, you can expect returns of between 10%, 15% or even 20%. However, when it comes to options, profit margins in excess of 1,000% are very possible.

We are familiar with bad investments and losses emanating from the actions of individuals or organizations that were hoping to be profitable. Numerous traders make huge errors when they trade resulting in major losses. This only happens when they know not what they are doing and when they do not take sufficient steps to protect themselves.

Remember that profits do not just show up. It takes plenty of hard work and most of all proper risk management techniques. Without risk management techniques in place, there is no need to enter the markets because you will be risking your funds. Keep in mind that trading options is a highly risky venture because it is speculative in nature. As such, you cannot trade without protecting yourself. Here are ways you can protect yourself and your trading capital.

1. Have a Trading Plan

This cannot be mentioned enough times. One of the most important things is to have a trading plan. This plan details exactly all the steps that you will follow from market entry to exit. You should sit down and consider all possible scenarios.

There is no need to take any risks. Once you learn as much as you can about options and trading, then you should learn how to plan your trades. Wise traders say anyone who fails to plan is planning to fail. If you want to succeed, then you should come up with a trading plan which you should then abide by. Again, there is no need of coming up with a trading plan if you will not implement it fully.

The main purpose of a trading plan is to ensure that you manage your money wisely and place it only well-planned and well-executed strategies. This way, you will avoid reckless moves and only put your money in strategies that are well worked out.

All too often, a trader will enter a trade without understanding exactly how it will play out. In such instances, the chances of losing money are extremely high. If you are unsure about any move, then please do not make it. A single move could imply a risk. With a good plan, all moves will be premeditated, and no unnecessary risks will be taken.

2. Understand Trading Psychology

Trading options largely revolves around three major factors. These are money management, trading strategies, and psychology. You need to keep in mind that the markets can be a very emotional place, so it is crucial that you remain focused and disciplined. If you do not stay disciplined, then you will lose out and others will very likely take advantage of you.

What you really need to do in order to trade successfully is to have a solid strategy, follow the strategy and stick to it. If the strategy does not follow the intended plan, then simply quit, and come up with another strategy.

If you have a strong mindset, you will be able to understand when to pursue a losing trade and when to quit. If you lack discipline, then one of two emotions will take over. These are greed and fear.

Sometimes traders trade on a whim and keep posting random trades. Rather than take this approach, you really should focus on a successful strategy which you will pursue until you need to exit. You should also have good trading skills and proper money management plan. With these in place, you will be able to focus better and think in terms of probabilities and risk-reward ratios. This way, you will not leave room for emotional trading.

There are other things that you need to also keep in mind. For instance, you need to develop and stick with good trading habits.

As a trader, you need to note that a winner is one who is persistent and consistent. You should develop the habit of closely studying the markets, conducting your analysis, and position sizing.

Position sizing is crucial, especially in a volatile market. As such, you need to take care of your downside risks and ensure that your position size appropriately. You should also envision the end game. Come up with a vision of where you want the trade to head then prepare to make any necessary adjustments.

You also need to accept any possible failures. Sometimes your strategies will not work out and you will lose some trades. This happens to all traders, even experienced ones. If you assume that you must succeed on each attempt, then you will be setting yourself up for failure.

3. Risks are Inherent

All types of investing opportunities carry a certain level of risk. However, trading options carries a much higher risk of loss. Therefore, ensure that you have a thorough understanding of the risks and always be on the lookout.

Also, these kinds of trades are very possible due to the nature and leverage offered by options. A savvy trader realizes that he or she is able to control an almost equivalent number of shares as a traditional stock investor but at a fraction of the cost. Therefore, when you invest in options, you can spend a tiny amount of money to control a large number of shares. This kind of leverage limits your risks and exposure compared to a stock investor.

4. Time is not on your Side

All options have an expiration date. When you invest in stocks, time is on your side most of the time. However, things are different when it comes to options. Basically, the closer that an option gets to its expiration, the quicker it loses its value and earning potential.

Options deterioration is usually rather rapid, and it accelerates in the last days until expiration. Basically, as an investor, ensure that you only invest dollar amounts that you can afford to lose. The good news though, is that there are a couple of actions that you can take in order to get things on your side.

Therefore, try and always or at least mostly to choose options whose expiry dates lie within your investment opportunity. Also, identify options that are at the money or very close. These increase your chances of profitability while minimizing risks and exposure. Ensure that you sell options whenever you believe that high prices are due to volatility. Instead, choose to purchase options when you believe that volatility is undervalued.

5. Naked Short Positions Can Result in Substantial Losses

Anytime that you decide to short options naked this presents a high likelihood of substantial and sometimes even unlimited losses. Shorting put naked means selling stock options with no hedging of your position.

When selling a naked short, it simply implies that you are actually selling a call option or even a put option but without securing it using an option position, stock, or cash. It is advisable to sell a put or a call-in combination with other options or with stocks. Remember that whenever you short sell a stock you are in essence selling borrowed stock. Sooner or later you will have to return the stock.

Fortunately, with options, there is no borrowing of stock or any other security.

6. Prices can Move Pretty Fast

Options are highly leveraged financial instruments. Because of this, prices tend to move pretty fast. Basically, options prices can move huge amounts within minutes and sometimes even seconds. T his is unlike other stock market instruments like stocks that move-in hours and days.

When structuring your options, you should ensure that you use the correct strike prices as well as expiration months in order to cut out most of the risk. You should also consider closing out your trades well before the expiration of options. This way, time value will not dramatically deteriorate.

CHAPTER 16:

How Do I Choose the Strike Price for Options Trading?

The strike price of an option is the price at which a put or call option can be exercised. It is otherwise called the exercise price. Picking the strike price is one of two key choices (the other being time to expiration) a financial specialist or trader must make while choosing a specific option. The strike price has a tremendous bearing on how your option trading will play out.

Strike Price Considerations

Accept that you have identified the stock on which you need to make an options exchange. Your subsequent stage is to pick an options strategy, for example, purchasing a call or composing a put. Then, the two most significant considerations in deciding the strike price are your hazard resistance and your ideal hazard reward result.

Hazard Tolerance

Suppose you are thinking about purchasing a call choice. Your hazard resilience ought to decide if you picked an in-the-money (ITM) call option, an at-the-money (ATM) call, or an out-of-the-money (OTM) call. An ITM choice has a higher affectability—otherwise called the option delta—to the price of the fundamental stock. If the stock price increments by a given sum, the ITM call would acquire than an ATM or OTM call. Be that as it may, if the stock value decays, the higher delta of the ITM option additionally implies, it would diminish in excess of an ATM or OTM call if the price of the fundamental stock falls.

Hazard Reward Payoff

Your ideal hazard reward result uses methods that measure the capital you need to chance on the exchange and your anticipated benefit target. An ITM call might be less dangerous than an OTM call; however, it costs more. If you just need to bet a modest quantity of capital on your call exchange thought, the OTM call might be the best, pardon the joke, option.

An OTM call can have a lot bigger increase in rate terms than an ITM call if the stock's floods past the strike price; however, it has a significantly less possibility of achievement than an ITM call. That implies, despite the fact that you plunk down a little measure of money to purchase an OTM call, the chances you may lose everything of your venture are higher than with an ITM call.

In view of these considerations, a relatively conservative financial specialist may choose an ITM or ATM call. Then again, a dealer with high resilience for hazard may incline toward an OTM call. The models in the accompanying area illustrate a portion of these ideas.

Picking the Wrong Strike Price

If you are a call or a put purchaser, picking an inappropriate strike price may bring about the loss of the full premium paid. These hazard increments when the strike price is set further out of the money. On account of a call essayist, an inappropriate strike price for the shrouded call may bring about the fundamental stock being called away. A few speculators want to compose somewhat OTM calls. That gives them a better yield if the stock is called away, despite the fact that it implies sacrificing some top-notch gains.

For a put trader, an inappropriate strike price would bring about the hidden stock being relegated at prices well over the present market price. That may happen if the stock dives unexpectedly, or if there is an abrupt market auction, sending most offer prices forcefully lower.

Strike Price Points to Consider

The strike price is an essential segment of making productive options play. There are numerous interesting points as you calculate this value level.

Have a Backup Plan

Options trading necessitate a considerably more active methodology than commonplace purchase and-hold contributing. Have a management plan prepared for your option trading, on the off chance that there is an abrupt swing in sentiment for a specific stock or in the wide market.

Time rot can quickly disintegrate the value of your long choice positions. Think about cutting your misfortunes and moderating venture capital if things are not going in your direction.

Evaluate Different Payoff Scenarios

You ought to have an approach for different situations if you plan to exchange options effectively. For instance, if you consistently compose secured calls, what are the reasonable adjustments if the stocks are called away, as opposed to not called? Assume that you are bullish on a stock.

Would it be progressively beneficial to purchase short-dated options at a lower strike price, or longer-dated options at a higher strike price?

The Bottom Line

Picking the strike price is a key decision for an option's financial specialist or trader since it has a significant effect on the gainfulness of an option. Getting your work done to choose the ideal strike price is an essential advance to improve your odds of success in options trading.

CHAPTER 17:

Leverage of Options: Double or Triple Your Returns.

Financial Leverage

The process of using borrowed capital (debt) to increase the shareholder's return on their investments or equity in capital structure is called financial leverage or Trading on equity. The financial leverage analyzed by the firm is intended to earn more return on the fixed charge funds rather than their costs. The surplus will increase the return on the owner's equity whereas the deficit will decrease the return on the owner's equity. Financial leverage affects the EPS (Earnings per share). When the EBIT increases, then EPS increases.

For example, if the firm borrows a debt from creditors for $1000 at 7% interest per annum i.e. $70 and invests this debt to earn a 12% return on this i.e. $120 per annum. Then the difference of surplus i.e. $50 which is after interest payment done to the creditors of the firm will belong to the shareholders or owners of the firm and it is referred to as profit from financial leverage. Conversely, if the firm would earn a 5% return, then the firm has a loss of $20 (i.e. $70 - $50) to the shareholders.

Highly leveraged companies may be at risk of bankruptcy if they are unable to make a payment on their debt, but it can increase shareholder's return on their investment and there are tax advantages associated with leverage.

Financial leverage ratio = EBIT / EBT

The financial leverage ratio is used to analyze the Capital structure and financial risk of the company.

It explains how the fixed interest-bearing loan capital affects the operating profit of the firm. If EBIT is more than EBT, this ratio becomes more than 1.

Types of Leverages

- Operating Leverage

Operating leverage is just concerned with the investment activities of an individual firm. It is about the incurrence of the fixed cost of operation in a company's income stream. The operating price can either be fixed, semi-fixed, variable as well as semi-variable. The fixed fee is contractual, and it is subjected to time. It does not necessarily have to change when the sales change, and it is supposed to be paid despite the number of sales.

- Financial Leverage

It is a relation to the combination of debts as well as equity in the capital format of a company. When there are financial charges in existence, the financial leverage will exist as well. The business costs should not depend on the operating profits in any way. The sources in which the funds that help to boost an investment come from can be put in categories.

The funds can either be having a fixed charge, and some may not be having the fixed financial cost. Debentures, preference shares, bonds as well as long-term loans have a fixed financial burden. Equity shares are known to have no fixed charge at all.

Combined Leverage

If you bring both the operating leverage and the financial leverage together, they will come up with the combined force. It is concerning the risk of one not being able to cover up for the total amount of the fixed charges. When a firm can cover fully on the operating as well as the financial burdens that is when the term combined leverage comes in. The higher the fixed operating cost as well as the financial charges, the higher the level of the combined force.

Working Capital Leverage

When there is a decrease in the investment of a particular asset, there will be an increase in profit. When there are many investors in the market and dealing with the same trade, there will be decreased profit. When there is a decrease in the investment of an asset, the risk associated with it will go high.

That means that risks, as well as returns, have direct relations. When the probability of risk goes up, there is a likelihood that the profit will increase as well. The ability of an individual firm to increase the effect of the change in the current stock on the firm's returns is working capital leverage. It is so when there is an assumption that the liabilities are constant.

The Risks of Incorrect Use

Limited Growth

When you have a loan, the lending company will expect that you will pay in the period that was agreed upon when you were getting the loan. They hope that you will be on time and no failures should come along the way. It is a problem when an investor borrows money for a long-term project that will not generate some income immediately. That will make them find an alternative to how they will pay the loan to avoid breaching the contract. If the payment period has come, and the investor has no returns, paying the mortgage can be a burden in one way or the other. When you decide to start paying the loan, it will mean that you use the money you borrowed to pay back. When that happens, you will have less money for financing your operations. You will not be in a position to implement full on the plan that you had. That means that you can have retardation, and you will not execute your plan fully. When investing, you need a plan and to set deadlines for the completion so that you will remain on your focus. When you have to pay the loan with the money that you borrowed, you will not be in a position to hit your deadlines. That will mean that you will experience limited growth, and you may not have the potential to continue as per the plan.

Losing Assets

When you are unable to pay loans, and you are highly leveraged, that can lead to a conspirator of the assets that you have. There is no way that a company should pay capital sourcing from equity. When that happens, and the lender expects that you will pay your loan in time, they can decide to take some of your assets to stand in for the loan. The assets can be of a similar value or a value higher than your investment. When in a loan, the company is supposed to pay the lender before any other deductions. Repossession of assets can happen if there is no money to pay the lender in time. It the lender has to be paid even before the employees of the company, it means that the employees may look for another option and quit working with you. That will make you lose assets of value, and you will be left stranded.

Inability to Get More Financing

Before a lender gives you money to invest in any trade, they will first check out whether you have any other loan. They will do that to establish how secure their payment is with you. If you are in debt, no lender will want to lend you more because they are not sure whether you will be in a position to clear their debt. They will access the risk that is associated in case the company goes down, meaning there will be no one to pay their loan. When a company goes down, it is declared bankrupt, and that means that the lender cannot claim their money even on a legal basis. No lender will agree to be put last on your loan list since they know they will be the last to be paid.

An Investor Will Not Be in a Position to Attract Equity

When a company has high leverage, they are not able to increase the equity capital amount. And it is rare for an investor to give money to a business that has bid records of unclear loans.

In the same way, lenders will avoid providing more money to a company with high amounts of investments, and the same way investors avoid such business. You will lose the potential of attracting investors when you have a lot of pending debts.

When a lender knows they are the last in your line to be paid, they will not find it logical to lend you. If at any chance you get an investor to give you money, they will demand a significant percentage in terms of ownership in return for borrowing you the money.

Advantages of Leverage

Increase in Profit

Leverage will earn you more benefits without necessarily having to put in more effort. Since it is borrowed money, you do not have to work so much so that you can earn it; instead, you look for a lender. When you fulfill the requirements, the lender will finance you and you will have to repay it back when the period lapses.

When you inject more capital into a business, it is likely to give you more returns under favorable market conditions.

An Increase in Capital Efficiency

When you increase the amount of money in a particular transaction it can lead to a rise in productivity on how you use your capital. You need to consider capital as an asset, and it can increase the level of yields. When you take a loan, you will increase the amount of money, and you will raise the level of efficiency.

As a Tool that Mitigates Against Low Volatility

Leverage is a great approach that can be put in place to mitigate the effect brought about by low volatility. Volatile trade is known to deliver huge profits in the Forex trade. It can deliver good benefits from a small transaction and can shield against the effect that comes with low volatility. A small entity can become a big firm with the help of leverage. Leverage will help you to capitalize on the small significant levels of movement in the trading price.

Disadvantages of Leverage

Lower Liquidity

It is worth noting that a lot of individual stock options have many volumes. There are cases where one is forced to own very few stocks.

The aspect that in all the options one has will trade at different strikes of payments as well as expectations. The particular option will be forced to have less volume unless it is one of the most popular stock indexes or stocks.

High Spreads

The art of lacking liquidity among these trading options causes higher spreads. The aspect is detrimental due to the fact that one is forced to pay more indirect costs while using trade options. The element is linked to the fact that when one is using the opportunity, they will be spreading the trade.

Higher Commissions

When one is operating with such organizations, one is forced to pay using commission terms. In other words, one has to pay a certain amount of commission for each dollar that is invested. The demerit is worsened by the fact that the option has very many possibilities that force one to have a lot of spreads.

CHAPTER 18:

How to Maximize Profits

You Can Profit from Any Market Situation

One can benefit from any market situation when trading options. Most options strategies are carried out by combining different option positions and sometimes even the underlying stock's position. A trading strategy can be used singly or in combination with others to profit from market situations.

[186]

You stand to make huge profits with options trading, yet your risk and exposure are limited. Ordinary stock trading does not afford you such opportunities. The most crucial aspects of options trading are to know when to exit a trade and how to exit. Knowing how and when to exit is vital for successful trading.

Options strategies are the most versatile strategies in the financial markets. They provide traders and investors with numerous profit-making opportunities with limited exposure and risk. These strategies can be favorable whether the stock price of the underlying security rises, remains the same, or falls.

Taking Profits with Options Trading

One of the best-known ways of profiting from options is through the purchase of undervalued options. You can even buy options at the right price and still benefit from them.

Options prices usually are extremely volatile. This provides an excellent chance to benefit from profit-taking. However, when you miss the right moment to take profits, you will have lost out on an amazing opportunity.

Take Advantage of Volatility and Collect Profits

Options are unlike stocks because they have a time limit. Stocks can be held indefinitely, but options can expire. This means that the time for trades is limited. As a trader, you cannot afford to miss this window. Should such a chance be missed, then it might not be seen again in a long while.

You should avoid long-term strategies when trading options. Strategies such as the average are unsuitable for options trading because of the limited time that options have. Also, watch out for margin requirements. Such requirements have the capacity to impact your trading funds requirements severely.

Watch out for multiple factors that may affect a favorable price. For instance, the price of the underlying stock may go up, which is a good thing. However, any accruing benefit may be eroded by other factors such as dividend payment, time expiration, or volatility. Such constraints make it imperative that you learn to follow profit-taking strategies. Here are some of these crucial profit-taking strategies that you can use as a trader.

Trailing Stop Strategy

When using this strategy, you will set a pre-determined percentage for a particular target. For instance, you can set ten options contracts with each costing $80 with a profit target at $100 and a $70 stop-loss.

Set a Profit-Taking Stop-Loss

You can set a stop-loss at 5%, which means if your target price of $100 is attained, your trailing target will be $95. If the upward trend continues and your price gets to $120, then the trailing target of 5% becomes $114. Should the price movement continue to, say, $150, then the trailing target this time becomes $142.5.

Should the price now start falling, you will exit and collect profits at $142.5. The trailing stop lets you enjoy protection as the price increases and then exit a trade once the price turns around.

The stop-loss levels should neither be too small nor too large. If they are too small, they will cause frequent triggers, whereas too large will make profit-taking unachievable.

Partial Profit Booking

Season traders have a routine that they follow to book partial profits. First, they set a target when to take profits when it is attained.

Partial profit booking helps to protect the trader's capital to a large extent.

This essentially has the effect of preventing capital losses in the event of a sudden price change. Such price reversals are commonly observed in options trading.

Book Partial Profits at Regular Time Intervals

As a trader, you can book partial profits at regular time intervals. However, you will need to pay close attention to the time limit.

A massive portion of your options premium is made of its time value. As time runs out, then its value also goes down.

As a trader, you should keep a keen eye on the time value of your options as this erodes their value. Buyers should be careful about the time limit.

Sell Covered Call Options Against Long Positions

Selling options is a lucrative income-generating process. This is not the only pathway to riches in the markets though. You can also sell naked puts. This is like selling shares or stocks that you do not own.

When you sell naked put options, you will free up your time to do a lot more. Stock trading allows you to sell stocks of shares that you do not have for a profit. This tends to free up your capital so you can invest it or trade with it indefinitely. It is advisable to stick to stocks that you understand very well and those you would not mind losing. There is still hedging associated with options trading, so always be careful and watch out about that. Most large investors who deal in options are often hedging.

Consider all the Options Available to You

We make assumptions that traders will hold their positions until the end. You can choose from several options to ensure that you can leverage any time you want to see its need.

Learn to Select the Right Options to Trade

You have to identify options that will see you earn a profit.

Make sure you determine whether you are bullish or bearish on the market sector, or just the stock. When you make these decisions, you will be able to identify the options you wish to buy.

Consider volatility and think about how it would affect your options trading strategy. Think about the status of the market. Is it calm, or is it volatile? You may also want to consider the expiration date and strike price. If you only have a couple of shares, this would be a great time and opportunity to purchase more stock.

Conclusion

Remember, that risk management is paramount. Always stick to your per trade risk figures and do not deviate from this no matter how attractive the setup might seem. Remember, the odds of success of a slam dunk looking setup and one that looks like a dog's dinner is the same. The market does not care about how pretty your setup is so neither should you. If the underlying conditions are fulfilled, you should execute your setup in the correct manner.

Your analysis should always begin with the technical market situation which is the order flow distribution and the trend or range situation. Often you will deal with trends with close to equal participation from both sides of the market. This should tell you that a reversal is probably imminent, and you should adjust accordingly.

Support and resistance will play an important role in determining where you ought to place your strike prices. Remember to evaluate support and resistance levels from an order flow perspective, instead of looking at every single available level on the chart. Look at the order flow characteristics the preceding time price made it there and compare it to the current order flow to get a feel for whether the level will hold or not.

Screening stocks is a straightforward matter if you follow the process outlined here. Compare the sector performance to the overall market performance to narrow down which sectors you ought to focus on. Once this is done, repeat the same process with individual stocks to select the best to speculate with.

Training and ending up with a loss or paying for training and earning profits? Well, it is entirely up to you to decide. What I can say is that having a mentor will prevent you from incurring unnecessary losses and result in a positive outcome.

Now that you are well equipped with the necessary information, it about time that you kick-start your journey in options trading. It is a good investment that can end with a favorable outcome. You know what it entails, its pros and cons, the option strategies, and tips for success. What else are you waiting for to start investing?

You should be in the process of opening a brokerage account as you start your journey as an options trader. It is currently the 'coolest' investment to start trading. Life comes with endless opportunities, and options trading happens to be one of them. If you are looking for an investment that will completely transform your life, this is it. It is a convenient, reliable, and fantastic way to generate additional income. Some people have made it a full-time job. This is because they have identified it as an investment that they can rely on for a successful outcome. If you are new in options trading, this is a perfect investment to carry out. The trick is to master the tactics that will increase your returns and minimize the risks. After all, the whole point of investing is to earn profits

There are a lot of different types of investments out there that you can choose to work with. Some are going to include taking over real estate and renting it out or selling it to others. Some will get into their own business and try to make money that way. And still, others will get into the stock market and hope they can make the right decisions. But one investment that is different from all the others is options trading.

This guidebook has taken the time to talk about options trading and all the neat things that you are able to do with it. We talked a bit about what options are and some of the benefits of choosing to work with them instead of with some of the other investments out there.

As with any investment type, there is some risk involved when you get into options trading. The good news is that you now know the most common mistakes to avoid and how to reduce the amount of risk that you take on with this investment opportunity. Options investing is a tricky investment to choose to go with, but it provides a great return on investment and is often easier to get into compared to the stock market

It is a good idea to put all of this into a trading plan in order to summarize your approach to the markets. Think of it as your trading business plan for success. List your instruments to trade, which strategies you will follow and how you will expand on them.

The topics covered here only scratch the surface with regards to trading options. There are a lot more strategies to consider. Your succeeding step would be to learn the Greeks and applying them in strategies.

I am not talking about the Iliad but the letters delta, theta, omega, alpha, and beta. You can also learn about ratio back spreads and butterfly trades. All of this sounds very exotic, but they are extremely effective.

However, before proceeding you should master the starter material in this book. The biggest problem for most traders is adjusting to the non-directional aspect of options. Understanding a stop loss and take profit is easy but dealing with a call option and a short put while experiencing a falling market tends to put their heads in a spin.

From novice to initiated, you have now gained the basics of knowledge that will help you enter the exciting world of options trading. It certainly is not everything there is to know, but you now have enough of a grounding to get started.

From here out, it is all about practice and being conservative as you improve your understanding and develop your own strategies. Only you will know what works best for you, how much risk you want to play with and how your personal ability to predict and determine the stock market can be best put into practice.

As you dip your feet into the water, you will start to see profits coming in and you will feel that buzz all options traders enjoy. The more you trade, the more you will see all these fundamental mechanics at play and the more you will start to connect the dots and figure out your own personality as a trader.

You are in for a treat – options trading is rewarding and exciting when done right. Remember to keep that calendar updated and to stay conservative at least in the beginning and you will enjoy that learning curve every step of the way!

Do not let one loss get you discouraged. The wealthiest traders and investors have all taken hits from which they thought they would never recover. Remember that you will have a few moments where you don't get as much back as you hoped but know that you will also have moments where you make more money than you ever did with your initial investment.

You have now had a careful stroll through the key standards and ventures in options trading we feel are fundamental to progress as an options trader. You have figured out how the options markets function, the best trading strategies and why it is basic to pick the best possible fundamental assets for the procedures you need to utilize.

You have additionally observed that great exit strategies are nearly as imperative as discovering great trades to enter, that focusing on the points of interest is basic, and that achievement is virtually inconceivable without a decent money-management plan—and the discipline to follow it.

At last, you have got lots of pages loaded with vital inquiries to consider in your search for the best online options broker. At the end of the day, it is a great opportunity to control, plug in—and profit. You have all the data to get 24-hour access to the options markets, fast and programmed execution of your orders and the most reduced commissions in the history of options trading. In any case, to share these advantages, you should be able to confront the lot bigger individual duties that accompany coordinate access to online trading.

You should have the discipline to do your very own research, screen your own positions and monitor every one of the points of interest you may leave to your full-benefit financial firm.

You can never again depend on a broker to watch your positions and call with guidance or suggestions. You are currently an autonomous administrator — and, all things considered, must be absolutely in charge of your own behavior.

You should likewise be mindful and be prepared to react to both fast moves in everyday trading designs and consistently evolving longer-term economic situations.

Thank you for reading this all the way through to the end! I hope that you have found this to be informative and educational.

Options are a great way to get in the stock market with a lot less upfront capital. They can be tricky because they come with expiration dates, so you must get in and out at the right time and cannot wait things out like you can with a stock.

But the return on investment is far superior to stocks when you make profitable trades. Be sure to study the securities that you are investing in carefully so that you know where the stock has real potential to move.

Also, keep learning, and I hope this was a good start.

Lightning Source UK Ltd.
Milton Keynes UK
UKHW022026080221
378458UK00003B/570